12/09/16.

Dear Bill

Thanks for stopping by. I hope you

enjoy! Best wishes,

THE No.1 BEST SELLER

First published as ebook and in paperback 2016
Copyright © 2016 Lee Bartlett
All rights reserved.
ISBN: 978-0-9955175-0-9

THE No.1 BEST SELLER

" A UNIQUE INSIGHT INTO THE MIND, STRATEGY AND PROCESSES OF A TOP SALESMAN "

LEE BARTLETT

I dedicate this book to my mum and dad for preparing me for all the challenges life has to offer, and to my beautiful little girl, Gigi, whose light will always be the brightest star in Daddy's universe.

Contents

Contents

Contents

Introduction

There are certain moments in life that always come to mind when you want to illustrate something very fundamental. Before I start this guide to how I became a top salesperson in one of the most competitive industries, let me go back to the day I met Timothy.

I was in the market for a new car. Having carried out extensive research, I decided on the model I wanted and found an ex-demo in stock at the main dealership with the exact specification I required. In many ways I had mentally and emotionally committed to buying it, so I wasted no time in booking a test drive. As the car was almost new, I was expecting simply to agree the details of the purchase soon after my arrival and take it home.

The showroom was plush and felt inviting as I walked in. I had parked directly outside the large glass-fronted doors but, as I approached the front desk, the woman whose primary function was to smile and greet customers did not look up for about ten seconds. "That's fine, if a little awkward," I thought. "But fair enough, she must be finishing some paperwork." When she did eventually acknowledge me, I stepped forward to explain I had an appointment. It was then that I noticed she had been reading a women's gossip magazine under the counter. So, within half a minute of entering, I couldn't help but feel a little undervalued. Especially as this was a dealership where the cheapest car in the showroom was £35,000 and I had just pulled up in an immaculate Porsche 911. In terms of hot prospects, I must have been in the top 1%.

She sat me down on the other side of the showroom and explained that the salesperson would be with me shortly. Well, I could see the salesperson at his desk and made eye contact with him on occasion, but he didn't acknowledge my presence for some 20 minutes. I was wondering if there had been some sort of mix up, so I went back to the reception and asked if there was somebody else that could set me up with a test drive. She walked over to the salesman who, having finished shuffling some papers on his desk, finally decided that he was now ready for me. He stood up, looked straight at me, and immediately contrived the most disingenuous smile I have ever seen. As he walked towards me, I couldn't help but notice his cheap shoes, tatty suit and dirty hair. He was like a caricature out of a spoof teenage movie and I felt more uncomfortable with his every step. When he had covered the 20 feet between us, he offered me his limp and excessively clammy hand which, when I shook it, had no resistance at all in its clasp. I found his overall lack of effort offensive.

He introduced himself as Timothy, and I couldn't help feeling a little ashamed in having to consider him a fellow salesperson. However, I immediately put my feelings aside and hoped he was at least good at his job. He ought to be, given his title of Senior Sales Executive. I gifted him a salesman's dream with my opening gambit. "Timothy, we spoke on the phone. I am here to test drive the car we discussed and take it home today. I presume you have worked out the trade-in deal for my Porsche. So, what have you come up with and how long will this process take?" Three sentences, pre-closing the deal for him and laying out my simple expectations. All he had to do, in order to generate rapport with me, was to make it look as though he had cut some sort of reasonable deal and make the process quick and straightforward.

Timothy explained that the car wasn't ready to be test driven, but that it would be available the next day as he wanted to ensure it had undergone the standard, prerequisite checks. I told him he had already had 24 hours to sort this out and asked why he hadn't called me to rearrange the appointment. To ensure that my trip wasn't entirely wasted, I wanted to at least flesh out the details of my trade-in and the purchase price, should the car meet my satisfaction. Timothy said that he was still waiting on a couple more quotes to ensure that he could offer me the best deal. I wasn't going to mention it at this point, but I would have been happy to pay cash for the car and sell my Porsche privately if he had made it worth my while – it couldn't have been easier for him. However, Timothy assured me that it would all be sorted by the next day. I noticed he was unapologetic for his failings but, still keen to buy the car, I agreed to return and start afresh.

The following day, all seemed fine. The receptionist was more responsive and Timothy greeted me upon my arrival. Of course, I was subjected to his smile again, but I was looking forward to jumping in the car and getting home. Timothy went to get the keys and transparently feigned surprise when he couldn't find them. It turned out that the car still hadn't arrived at the showroom. He explained this, and I explained to him, very concisely, how poor my experience had been so far. I told him that he needed to go and get the car *now* if he wanted to make a sale. I had spent an hour getting to the showroom on two consecutive days and their treatment of a potential customer wasn't acceptable. Timothy then went on to explain that he still hadn't heard back on the quotes for my Porsche. He promised me that, if I came back in two hours, all would be sorted. So I decided that, rather than wait around, I would use the time to visit another luxury car showroom in the area. I immediately liked the salesperson at the new garage and ended up really liking another car that I hadn't even considered. This helped me disengage from the first car and opened my mind to an alternative. I returned to Timothy's showroom far less interested in being there or even in buying the car, which was finally ready. The car was nice and another salesperson took me for the test drive. He was more on the ball than Timothy and, although I was not as excited as before, I still reckoned I would buy it.

I was expecting to be able to finalise the deal when I returned to the showroom but had decided, regardless of the offer, that I would consider it over the weekend before committing. I wanted Timothy to sweat a bit for making it such an unpleasant experience. Needless to say, when I returned after the test drive, Timothy still hadn't completed any of the paperwork, but he promised a formal proposal would be emailed to me that evening. My frustration peaked; I insisted on seeing the dealership sales manager and detailed the poor performance of his sales staff. He promised to ensure a smoother process going forward.

Timothy's proposal never did arrive and, after a cooling off period that weekend and a more professional experience from the competing dealership, I decided to buy the car from them. I considered writing a letter to Timothy's management explaining the diabolical series of events that resulted in the loss to them of a £45,000 sale — but decided against it. I felt a far better punishment would be to let them continue trading in this way.

As a matter of fact, the second salesperson who had stepped in to take me for the test drive had told me that I was "in good hands" with Timothy as he was their resident product expert and *top salesman*. This blew my mind, and made me want to re-examine my own feelings towards Timothy because, as far as I was concerned, he had failed on every single level. What had he done so wrong? Was it that he was treating me how he would like to have been treated? Perhaps waiting a few days to buy a car would have been no big deal to him and that he thought I should be more relaxed about it. Maybe sending a proposal a few days late meant as little as leaving a customer hanging on for 20 minutes or so in a showroom before being introduced to the salesperson. Equally, perhaps, he would have been more understanding if it were he who was buying a car that wasn't ready as promised, because it was undergoing last-minute quality control checks. After all, in his mind, maybe it really showed that they were thoroughly checking the vehicle before sale.

It is also possible that he didn't apply any standard sales processes to me because, in his experience, his customers are all high net worth individuals who don't typically appreciate sales techniques. Moreover, if Timothy really was a top salesman, maybe he dressed down because he didn't want to flaunt his success in the showroom. It was all possible. I will return to Timothy's true failings, however, at the end of this introduction.

We all know a Timothy and have experienced poor salesmanship. In many regards, I sometimes feel that poorly executed sales processes have become the norm, and I often despair when dealing with the average salesperson and their lack of pride in providing the best product or service. However, the purpose of this book is not to focus on the poor performance of others; rather it is to describe what makes a top salesperson different from their colleagues. Specifically, I want to share the things that I have done – differently from others – which have ensured that I have always been the dominant salesperson across a variety of different roles throughout my career.

From the very beginning, when I landed a chance job in telesales, I quickly rose up the ladder to work in consultative, enterprise and, later, more cut-throat transactional sales environments. During a diverse career, mainly focused on selling financial technology, I have held sales roles in large US, UK and European-based corporations, and have sold extensively across most countries in these regions, as well as in Asia. The benefit of such varied experience is that I am able to compare the underlying styles and sales approaches of different organisations and cultures, and to share the most effective sales strategies of each.

The nucleus of this book is Chapter 2: The Basics. This describes the key differences in my approach, which led at one time to establishing myself as the highest grossing individual globally in my industry. The product I sold had few distinguishing features from a competitive standpoint, so the key determinant behind this result was pure positioning and salesmanship. My clients were C-Suite executives and professionals from the most prestigious investment banks in the world, and the deals were often high value, with an extremely short lead-time from first contact to securing the mandate. I couldn't have reached this pinnacle of sales success without doing something a little extra than my colleagues or competition, and in each role I refined my own set of learnt skills and applied them with the utmost precision.

> **❝ ...the key determinant behind this result was pure positioning and salesmanship.**

Dominant salespeople in any organisation are, by definition, shrewd individuals with a natural instinct for finding and closing deals at the maximum price. These top salespeople understand better than any of their peers the mechanisms by which to sell their products or services. They place themselves within the most pertinent information flows in order to source deals, and they strive to meet all the influencers and decision-makers to understand what each expects from the service being offered. In closing they are then able to convey a powerful message: I understand your requirements, my organisation, with my guidance, is best suited to meet those requirements, and I am passionate about working with you. Put simply, through rigorous preparation, a top salesperson somehow wins deals from the offset and makes the art of being a salesperson look deceptively easy as they consistently generate more revenue than anyone else.

Novice and mediocre salespeople often dismiss the skill of top performers as luck or put it down to natural talent. I acknowledge that having these traits does help. But in my 15 years of selling and competing against the best in any of the industries, it has become clear that it is more than natural talent that keeps the few of us at the top. Rather, I know that success comes from a rigorous combination of trained mind-sets, drive and methodology, which result in an ability to read clients, understand the decision-making matrices and know instinctively when and how to close. With the exception of an individual's innate drive, which is a critical component of success, all of these skills can be developed over time and I certainly did not possess them at the beginning of my career. It is also often said that sales success is primarily based on whether your product is better than the competition. Again, it certainly helps – but I have proved many times that a superior salesperson can often sell an inferior product.

Granted, people have lucky years or find themselves on massive deals just because they are in the right place at the right time, but to stay at the top of their game through good times and bad, a salesperson must be consistently doing something right. On the subject of luck, I consider the luckiest aspect of my career to be that I have been able to learn from, and emulate, some really great salespeople, many of whom I refer to in this book.

I have been asked many times to share my secret to consistent sales success. I tend to pacify most people with a simple one or two sentence answer but, of course, I know such a short explanation can never be truly adequate. For example, I have sometimes told people that the key to my success is, "I simply treat my clients exactly how I would want to be treated." I do believe this, but as Timothy has kindly allowed me to demonstrate, there is a twist in the interpretation of this statement that most salespeople miss. In the first place, there isn't a person to whom I have said this who hasn't agreed with me or felt they could connect with the statement. There's an obvious truth at its core and, to most salespeople, it usually results in the satisfactory end of the conversation. This has always suited me because, before writing this book, I had never wanted to share or discuss my sales approach with my peers.

However, if the truth of the statement is so obvious,

then why do so few salespeople appear to act on it? The complexity of the truth behind this statement is that everyone's personality and standards are unique. What I have observed, however, both in myself and in other top salespeople, is that our standards are based on perfection in every aspect of our sales approach and this, most importantly, includes adopting a sales process based entirely on the needs and standards of our prospect or client. Without exception, I visualise every aspect of client contact from *their* perspective. With this in mind, a more correct statement would be, "I treat my clients as they wish to be treated." This statement is, however, prone to discussion and, in the past, that's something that I have tried to avoid.

I have also been known to tell people that I work harder than my colleagues, execute the same basic sales process on every prospective client, or talk to more people than anyone else. Others

> **"** ...success comes from a rigorous combination of trained mindsets, drive and methodology.

sometimes get, "It's not so much what I do that is the key to my success but, rather, what other salespeople don't do that allows me to close deals." Again, all this is seemingly fairly straightforward conceptually but, as you may by now be beginning to understand, these aphorisms have much deeper connotations. I will be addressing my interpretation of each of them throughout this book.

Writing this book has required an enormous amount of self-analysis and reflection in order to share my approach to selling in a structured manner. This process has highlighted the fact that, in many ways, I view my role as a sales professional very differently from my colleagues. I want to start with a principle that resonates through all that I have to say – to make it very clear how I measure sales success. My definition is quite simply how much money hits my bank account. So, the top salesperson is the person who earns the most. It is not the person who is praised the most or who is the highest revenue generator for the company – unless they are also the highest paid. At the most basic level, this means that I don't consider a sale to be closed until the commission hits my bank account, and this mindset ensures that I maintain the same exemplary service throughout the entire sales cycle.

> **❝ ...the top salesperson is the person who earns the most.**

Similarly, my definition of hitting target is that of achieving my own personal financial goal, and not necessarily that of the company. My aspirations are always greater than those of my employer, and by focusing on a personal goal, independent to that of the company, I feel that I am able to operate with a clearer sense of purpose. This allows me to minimise my emotional response to the many non-revenue generating distractions that are so often present in highly driven and political sales environments. Everything I do in the office and in my role as a salesman is channelled towards my goal, from the products that I choose to sell and the contract negotiated before I join, to my day-to-day activities. This unfaltering commitment to personal success is a common intrinsic trait that I share with other top salespeople I have met throughout my career.

This book is not intended to be an instruction manual. There are many different types of sales positions and team structures, so what I write will not apply in its entirety to every sales professional. Neither do I claim to know, or to have attempted to list, every aspect of sales technique. What follows is simply an honest reflection of my early career selling technology platforms and services to the financial markets with the aim of sharing what I did differently that kept me at the top of the game. It is divided into four sections, which collectively build up to a description of the full methodology.

The first section describes the key markers for how I choose a company and product to sell. Product selection has always been key to my success. If the selection is not made in a structured and quantified manner, then it will not support the mechanisms that will allow me to exceed my sales targets. *The Basics* describes the things I learnt to do that have always kept me at the top of my profession. The third section focuses on the various, and often unspoken, obstacles that have hindered my path to success and that experience has taught me to manage. Finally, the fourth section highlights many important aspects of negotiating a sales-based employment contract. There is also a free audio download to accompany the section "Product evaluation and pitch preparation", whereby I articulate a previous pitch to demonstrate some of the principles that I have described.

However, before I begin, let's revisit Timothy. When you read the story about his performance from the buyer's perspective it becomes very clear how poorly the sales process was conducted. I am glad to say that I just don't have the personal capacity to treat anybody in the way in which Timothy and his colleagues treated me. On the most basic, human level, I consider it completely indecent to ignore someone or not communicate with them when commitments are being broken. My high standards are part of my personality and upbringing and, combined with rigorously applied sales techniques, results in a whole package that has proved to be a potent recipe for sales success. However, Timothy's deficit in this department is not what cost him the sale.

Whether Timothy felt his sales approach would have been acceptable to him is completely irrelevant because he wasn't the one looking to part with £45,000. If he did feel this, then he has made the same mistake as other below average salespeople. They fail because they cannot

THE NO.1 BEST SELLER

put their egos to one side and bother to understand that selling a product is about the customer and not about them. Timothy then is the antithesis of everything I believe is acceptable in sales, but he certainly isn't unique.

I have seen many such characters throughout my career. In one respect, people like Timothy have made my job easier over the years, and I have won countless mandates only to hear from my client afterwards just how poorly my competition conducted themselves, or how little they understood the client's requirements. Timothy's promises were as genuine as his smile. I instinctively tuned into his insincerity from the outset, which is why I did everything in my power to make the transaction end as quickly as possible. I knew the process was going to be a bind because he didn't respond to the very first thing I said to him, which laid out the deal on a plate.

Maybe Timothy was the top salesman for this dealership, but I can guarantee that he wouldn't have been if I had worked there – and he would be lucky to have lasted a single day in some of the environments in which I have worked. So what, exactly, cost Timothy this deal? His real failing, and the thing that turned a guaranteed sale into a loss, was that he didn't acknowledge or care about *my needs and expectations* as a buyer – despite my having spelled them out for him at the very beginning.

As a top salesman for my entire career, I can say of the

25

literally thousands of people to whom I have pitched, that I understood exactly how every single one of them wanted to be treated. It's a bold statement and it must be hard to imagine which cutting-edge sales technique I employ to ascertain this privileged and key information. Well, after a firm handshake and a short introduction, if my potential customer hasn't told me what they want, as I told Timothy, ***then I just ask.***

Section 1

How I pick a
product to sell

"Train hard, fight easy..." I heard this in my local boxing gym as a boy and it made perfect sense. Since that moment, I have always tried to over prepare in everything I do – and never more so than when picking a product to sell.

Over the course of my career, it became clear that my efforts alone could never be enough to hit my goals consistently. All products must have the necessary foundations upon which to build success: a great customer service team that share a common goal for excellence, an adequate budget to finance growth, and a management team with the experience and vision to ensure that opportunities are utilised. Understanding whether these mechanisms are in place before joining a company requires extensive research on many levels. Furthermore, it's not enough just to look internally at how the company operates; it is equally important to understand the market, and whether the product, as brilliant as it may be, actually fills a need within the target community.

I always seemed to have had a natural instinct for selecting the right products to sell. This may be because I never viewed the concept of work as a fun activity that just took up the majority of my day for 45 years of my life. Rather, going to work was little more than an opportunity to earn the maximum amount of money possible to make my life easier and more secure. With this in mind, I have always sought products and employers that offered me the maximum rate of return for what I viewed as the *investment* of my time. The product and the intricacies of selling it were never a concern to me, because that can always be learnt. I just looked for *maximum potential* and based all my research prior to joining a new company on understanding this. Should all the prerequisite factors align, then my commitment has always been absolute and focused entirely on achieving my personal financial goal.

Just as any good investor does extensive research based on a set of criteria before acquiring an asset, when picking a product I have a set of *ten* personal key markers that experience has shown will put me in the best possible position to succeed. Get it wrong at this stage and you are setting yourself up to fail, no matter how a good a salesperson you might be. I have never left any company because there was an issue with selling my product. There has always been an external factor outside of my contribution that has had a deal-breaking influence on my work life. So, in my opinion, the key to product and employer selection is not only being able to recognise opportunities as they arise, but also not overlooking the non-sales related obstacles that can hinder success.

In addition to my key markers for product selection, I also want to describe how I have managed to re-establish myself on two separate occasions in collapsed markets after periods of extended absence. It is at times like these when true resolve is tested and product and company selection is paramount.

The best way to share how I learnt to do all of this is to describe chronologically the initial 15 years of my career, with a focus on my reasons for joining, as well as leaving, each of my five employers. By analysing my thought processes and the experiences from each, I will demonstrate how I learnt to identify the key characteristics for successful product selection, as well as assessing the credibility of the company that supplies it. What is interesting about this entire journey is that, on multiple occasions, the same lesson needed to be learnt a number of times before it stuck.

GETTING STARTED

In the beginning, launching into the world of work was simple because there was no choice. Having recently graduated from university on the South Coast of England, I was immediately offered a job with a pharmaceutical company as a research scientist for £14,000 per year, but my aspirations were far greater than standing in a laboratory mixing chemicals. Like many before, I headed to London to try to understand how people earned big money. Heavily in debt and with one month's rent in my pocket, I needed to get a job quickly to survive. A friend offered to put me up on her sofa for a week, giving me enough time to source a tiny room near the middle of town and search for work. At the local job centre there was an advertisement for stacking bookshelves that paid £10 per hour, which seemed a lot, so I applied and was hired the next day. It was a part-time role so it freed up my time to look for a more permanent and meaningful position. I wasn't sure what type of role or profession to look for but my goal was very clear – to earn a lot of money.

I scoured the appointment sections in the newspapers every day and applied for many positions, interviewing with several recruitment companies. However, dealing with the agencies was a total misery because very few would put me forward for a position because of a lack of experience. Then, one evening I arranged to go out for a beer with my brother and his friend who worked for a company in the financial industry as a magazine salesman. I explained to him how frustrating it was finding a decent role after graduating and how my financial situation was becoming precarious. He was a really nice guy and we talked about his job and what it involved. He explained that in its most basic form you called up someone who worked in an investment bank and asked them if they wanted a free copy of your magazine, which was specific to their profession. Then you called them back a week later and, if they liked it, asked them if they would like to subscribe. It sounded so easy, but the best bit was that his salary was related to his performance, so the more people who subscribed, the more he earned.

The consistent conversion of leads to sales per month was approximately 2%, so if he made more calls he could quite accurately predict his increase in earnings. His basic salary was little more than I was earning in my part-time position, but the best salespeople doubled their basic salary every month. Nobody had ever explained a sales role to me like this before, and this guy was nothing like my idea of the stereotypical salesperson. He said he couldn't promise but he should be able to get me an interview as they were always looking to hire good people. However, it was up to me whether or not I landed the job. It sounded great, and despite knowing nothing of sales or finance, I did know that, given the opportunity to have a performance-related salary, I would work harder than anybody else on the planet. Also, the job was based in the financial district of London, and this is where the bulk of the wealth seemed to reside. Suffice to say, with a little guidance from my new friend and a lot of background reading on the company, its products and the industry, I was hired after three interviews. I had just stepped on to the first rung of the ladder.

It just so happened that I had landed a job with a highly driven sales team that also provided superb training. The company was a large US corporate and my office was their European headquarters. They were the market leader in the provision of financial data to investment banks and corporate law firms in the city. During my interview it was explained that my role was to sell one of the lowest grossing magazines in the portfolio, but it was a product that they felt had more potential. My manager was frustrated that the salespeople currently selling the product were not particularly hungry and, as a result, were not making the most of their opportunity. They were earning approximately half their basic salary in commission each month, but with more effort and the right person, the expectation was that the current sales could easily double.

It was a great opportunity and I was fired up to get going. The first month was spent in training, which included multiple aspects of sales such as lead generation, basic closing techniques, negotiation and, importantly, how the financial industry worked. I had an insatiable appetite to understand my client and why they needed our product. Importantly, as a rookie salesman, I knew my place and did exactly as I was told.

Around this time, I started to understand sales pipelines and targets, so decided to set a personal goal and calculate how many sales it would take to repay my student loans. To do this quickly meant grossing £3,000 per month or, in other words, earning the equivalent of my basic salary in commission. The commission rate was a straight 10% of gross sales and the magazine sold for £575 per year, so I needed 26 sales per month. This broke down into 22 working days per month, which translated into one sale per day plus one bonus sale per week. To hit this number would require approximately 80 phone calls per day, which, with a 2% conversion rate, would yield an average 1.6 sales per day or 35 sales per month. Factor in that there would be customers procrastinating and changing their mind, there was still a nine sales per month buffer to hit my personal commission target of £1,495 which, combined with my basic salary of £1,500 per month, resulted in total compensation of £2,995. It was a very basic calculation that didn't take into consideration a number of other important factors such as total potential market sizing or level of product adoption within my assigned territory, but the purpose of this calculation was twofold. Firstly, it gave me a mental target to aim for and a clear path to pay off my loans. Secondly, it demonstrated to my new boss how hard I was prepared to work. On review, he seemed to enjoy my plan and explained that the average telesales rep made 55 calls per day, between 9am and 5.30pm.

The good news for me was that the bankers who would be interested in my product typically worked until very late so there was no barrier to achieving my call volumes. Also, despite being well known in the UK market, my product had barely been sold to European institutions, so it had an almost endless potential across continental Europe, the Middle East and Africa. The company provided an unlimited source of leads, which would consist of qualified client enquiries and individuals specific to the industry. Finally, delivering the call and sales numbers in my plan would place me at the top of the sales board and represented 200% of my "in house" target per month, which was 13 sales or £7,475 of revenue. My new boss was talking my language. He was worthy of being looked up to because he was very confident and successful, with an engaging personality.

Being top of the sales statistics was great, and every new subscription increased my motivation. Quickly learning the schedules of my clients, I devised a work strategy that staggered my breaks to coincide with theirs, making it easier to catch them at their desks. The most productive part of the day was after my colleagues left at 5.30pm because the office was silent and it was easier to focus. Putting in 12-hour shifts ensured that I always delivered on my numbers plus a little extra, and I was soon noticed within the organisation as a rising talent. After just four months, my student loans were paid off. Around this time, it came to my attention that the company was about to launch a new magazine into the Asian market. It was not hard to see that this was my next big opportunity.

The publication was earmarked for a more experienced salesperson in the team but I had to have it – for two reasons. First, being a new publication it was virgin territory, so with a strong pitch I could expect high sales volumes. Second, Asia is a different time zone so I could sell my current magazine until mid-afternoon and then focus on Asia all night. My commitment to the company was irrefutable in terms of call statistics and, after several meetings to convince both the magazine editor and the sales manager, they eventually conceded that the responsibility for selling this new publication should be mine. It proved to be a golden period, and over the following months I worked exhaustively to earn a sum of money I could only have dreamed of prior to joining.

In the meantime, it was clear that, in order to advance my career, my role as a salesman was equally important internally within the company as it was externally to clients. If my boss was talking to divisional managers, then I always made an effort to get an introduction. My strategy of learning not only about my division but also the company as a whole was getting me noticed at all levels.

My next break came quite quickly when my boss had a substantial promotion to another division. He was made Head of Sales for a team of consultant salespeople. The team was reshuffled and a number of them, many with over ten years of sales experience, decided to leave the company. This left a hole that needed to be filled, and I was invited to interview as a junior salesman within the new team. This was unprecedented: with just six months sales experience, I was the only person from the telesales team asked to apply. My boss recognised how hard I was prepared to work in order to learn the necessary skills to advance, so he went out on a limb to get me hired.

My basic salary suddenly doubled and my earning potential increased four-fold. I was sent on a series of more advanced sales training courses as this new role was no longer just telesales but field-sales based, a change that really excited me. Also the lead-time on a sale was a little longer than the week-long trial period that was offered to a potential magazine subscriber. The job had changed from calling clients on the phone to visiting more senior prospects and presenting my products in person. To begin with it was nerve-racking to present to groups, but I ensured I booked four meetings a day and after a short time it became second nature. I was 22, succeeding beyond all expectations on the sales front and had saved enough to put down a deposit on my first home.

Approximately six months into this new role, my boss scheduled some time with me for a review. Things were going well, but he had news about some imminent changes to the structure of the company. The main impact on me was that three divisions of the company were about to be merged and rebranded into one entity. This meant that a number of salespeople would be leaving the company and a more streamlined team would be left to sell the three products of the combined entity. He explained it was a golden opportunity for me as I would be a fully-fledged consultant selling a suite of the company's flagship products. I would also be the youngest team member by some 10 years and had reached the top of this company's sales force in just under 18 months.

Even though quickly advancing to sell more complex platforms was a blessing in terms of sales experience, this was not the case when they presented the new associated commission packages. Until now my remuneration was simply a percentage of revenue, but it didn't work this way under the new structure. It stands to reason that, when tasked to sell three different products, they are not likely to be in equal demand. It took me years to be able to truly articulate this, and it is concisely illustrated in the Product Adoption Curve presented below:

WHERE DOES MY PRODUCT LIE ON THE PRODUCT ADOPTION CURVE?

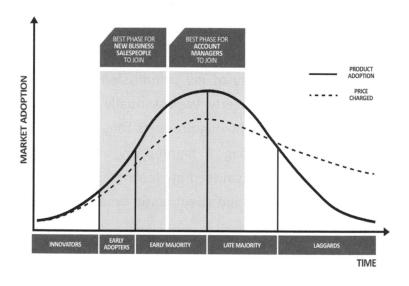

The curve correlates two important relationships. Firstly, it demonstrates the relationship between a product first entering the market and its associated adoption as it matures. Secondly, it explains the relationship between the price of the product relative to its adoption in light of new players entering the market. These two factors are *absolutely* key when reviewing new products to sell, and their position on the adoption curve is my first and most fundamental consideration.

At the time I had little understanding of the problem, but in hindsight two of my inherited products were on the downward trend of the curve. Yet my original product was in far more demand and on the upward trend. No problem, you would think – just focus on selling the product in most demand. Unfortunately, my new commission structure incentivised against this. I had to sell all three platforms in equal proportion; otherwise no commission payment was due at all. To support this scheme the frequency of my commission was moved from monthly to quarterly. We essentially had to force clients to commit to buying products they didn't really want, and it felt wrong. It blunted my drive, but the management team dismissed my feelings. I stuck it out for six more months and spent some time considering other offers.

I had progressed from a graduate with no sales experience to having sold seven different products for three divisions of one of the world's largest US-based providers of financial data. The company had trained me to operate at a level that was ten years ahead of my age, and my sales results and learnt skill set enabled me to legitimately tackle the most senior of sales positions elsewhere in the industry. In addition, my salary had increased fivefold since starting. Was this all down to luck? You could argue there was an element of luck, but without delivering more revenue than my more experienced peers at every stage of the process I would not have been able to progress. I believe I created my own luck by being in the mix and working harder and smarter than anybody else.

WHAT TYPE OF SALESPERSON AM I?

The period of reviewing new companies and products was a useful time to reflect on the type of salesperson I had become. It was clear that I thrived on the challenge of contacting new prospects and selling as much of a product as possible. The industry definition for this type of salesperson is a New Business Salesperson (NBS). If a NBS sits at one end of a spectrum, the other end would suit someone who likes to service accounts and maintain existing relationships with the aim of renewing business when a contract expires. These Account Managers tend to have a different personality type and are much better suited to working with a more mature product that is nearer the apex of the Product Adoption Curve. American corporations commonly refer to NBSs and Account Managers as *hunters* and *farmers*. A balanced sales team has a mix of both characters, but certainly in my younger years I was a pure hunter and my motivation to sell was deeply rooted in doing as many deals and making as much money as possible.

Understanding the type of salesperson I had naturally become was the first step in deciding which opportunities to pursue. Not only did any new product need to suit my personality type, but I also wanted to improve my knowledge and experience, as well as earn more money. My three requirements in considering any new role were clear:

KEY MARKER #1

WHERE DOES THE PRODUCT LIE ON THE PRODUCT ADOPTION CURVE?

As I was a pure New Business Salesperson, my next product had to be a new concept or technological release, and therefore positioned low on the adoption curve so that I could ride the crest of new business uptake as well as the associated ability to charge the highest price. I was clearly best suited to covering a large territory and convincing potential new clients to buy a product or service.

KEY MARKER #2

DOES THE PACKAGE MEET MY SALARY EXPECTATIONS?

My salary had risen dramatically over the previous 18 months and I had come to learn my value. Also, I had heard stories of salespeople in my industry joining fledgling products and earning massive commission payments, so I wanted find one of these opportunities for myself. The market was strong; I was at the top of my game and working for an industry leading company, so wouldn't consider a move without at least a 50% upside on my current salary.

KEY MARKER #3

WHAT AM I LEARNING THAT WILL
MAKE ME BETTER?

Despite my success, I was still young and had a lot to learn, so ideally I wanted to work for someone who could take me to the next level.

It wasn't long until a call came from a headhunter with a very loud, grand voice, telling me I had come to the attention of a small UK-based financial data provider who were looking to launch a new product. The product was one of two in the market and, although it wasn't the dominant product at that time, it was undergoing a complete overhaul. The new release had the potential to become the market leader and the client base mirrored many of my existing accounts. It sounded interesting so I agreed to a meeting and immediately connected with the Sales Director. He explained that he too had come from a large US corporate to run the launch of the new product and was looking to hire the cream of the industry.

The fact that he had resigned from running one of the most successful sales teams in the City to join this company legitimised the opportunity. I was being offered the chance to be a part of, to learn from, and to pitch myself against a team of highly experienced and driven sales professionals. We discussed salary and the numbers were simple. He offered a small increment on my basic salary to entice me to join, but my focus was firmly rooted in the potential upside.

The commission rate was a clean 10% of deal value, with the average deal expected to sell for £20,000 to £30,000. The product had a one- to three-month sales cycle inclusive of appropriate trial periods and my target was £1million per year or £85,000 per month.

Crunching the numbers and taking my basic retainer into consideration, this put me 50% over my current salary. In addition, there was a superb incentive in the form of a commission accelerator for achieving in excess of 100% of my sales target, whereby my commission rate on this incremental revenue began to increase. This was highly appealing to me because company new business targets are, in my opinion, the minimum amount of business a salesperson must generate and they always sit firmly below my own personal target. The icing on the cake was that none of the major accounts were yet subscribers to this new product and, despite being the youngest member of the team, my experience and client relationships were already more relevant than those of either of the two existing salespeople. As a consequence, I decided to try my luck and proposed an account deck prior to joining that was literally a list of the top 20 investment banks and law firms in the City. To my surprise, the majority of these were assigned to me and it felt almost too good to be true. The last thing to do was ask a handful of trusted clients what they thought of this new product and if it fitted with their business plans. The feedback was very positive in regard to my potential new employer, so I accepted the role without hesitation.

The two salespeople who had joined prior to my arrival had already begun to approach clients and sign business. One of them was a highly experienced salesperson and, having closed a good-sized contract in the short period since arriving, was already firmly established at the top of the sales ladder. It was puzzling to me, though, that both these so-called top salesmen, with all their years of experience, seemed to have missed the biggest trick. Either, they just weren't that smart, or they hadn't done their homework before joining because, when offered at interview stage to list their desired accounts, neither had chosen the most obvious revenue generators.

On being introduced to the leading salesman, my first impression was that he was a little condescending. I found this interesting because we shared the same job title. He strode arrogantly around the office as if he owned the place and spoke with an air of insincerity as if considering every syllable. This didn't sit well with me, and I decided within ten seconds of meeting him that I was going to annihilate his sales records. In fact, I knew with absolute conviction that I was going to dominate the entire sales team despite my age and no matter whom they hired.

I hit the ground running, bringing all my old sales processes with me. This was a different product though, which required me to temper my aggressive style, which was typical of someone who had trained in a large US corporate sales team. My boss had trodden the same path and was able to guide me through a slightly different and more interpersonal sales approach. I learnt to be aggressive in my approach, not my manner, but nothing short of massive success would quench my desire to prove myself the superior salesperson and maximise my earning potential.

The next two years were taken up with work and little else, often generating revenues over double that of my monthly target. My reputation as the top salesman was percolating through the industry and life was good. The only problem was that the majority of my account deck was now contracted into 12–24 month commitments, so the product was fast approaching the apex of the adoption curve. I had become a victim of my own success; my role was changing more to account management, and that didn't suit me.

The company had provided me with an incredible opportunity to further develop the skills of selling enterprise solutions. Unfortunately, though, it only specialised in the provision of one product and, with little potential to develop its content or features in the short term, I had outgrown my role. It was only ever a two-year tenure, as this was the length of time it took me to take my accounts from new business to contracted revenue.

KEY MARKER #4

IS THERE PROGRESSION ONCE MY PRODUCT HAS MATURED?

Longevity in any sales role is directly related to how long the product is able to meet my personal requirements. When considering future sales positions, I would be sure to consider this from the outset.

I was 25 years old, and my desire to travel, and to do it in style while still young, was getting the better of me. My inclination was to leave the industry for a while, but I was advised against leaving a bull market while still at the top of my game. Being young, brash and feeling invincible, I didn't really care what people were saying, and after two of the most amazing years working at this company, my life had consisted of little more than client meeting rooms and the four corners of an office. I knew it was reckless but decided there was more to life and took off on a global adventure.

RE-ESTABLISHING YOURSELF IN A COLLAPSED MARKET

The year off ended up closer to two years. During this time, I was totally out of the loop, exploring the Asia-Pacific region and the US, and had blown an enormous amount of my available cash. When I left, the housing market in the UK was booming and I had decided to place my newly acquired home on the market to cash in on the capital gains. In addition, my equity portfolio was heavily weighted in technology stocks, and shortly after I left for distant shores the bubble burst. Roll 9/11 into this, and the markets I found on my return were a shadow of what they had been in previous years. I had never experienced an economic downturn before, so I never considered that it might impact my ability to re-enter the job market and earn big money once again.

Frustratingly, the average property price had all but doubled, but I needed somewhere to live so I bought an apartment in central London with my remaining equity and focused on starting again. I began contacting a number of people in the industry in an attempt to discern the next big product or service about to break into the market. The consensus was very negative. A lot of people had been laid off in the financial industry; revenues were down for all firms, and deal volumes a fraction of what they had been. We were in a downward economic spiral and companies were trying to hold on to their revenue streams and cut back budgets. There were still the standard mundane sales roles with the big firms, but despite feeling the pressure I needed to choose my next position carefully and wait for the right product. I spent some time with my parents and kept in touch with friends in the industry who kept me informed of developing trends. This paid dividends, as one day an ex-client and good friend of mine at a leading corporate law firm said he had been approached by a company that was pitching an interesting new technology product.

This was a new concept called a Virtual Data Room, which streamlined the process of reviewing highly confidential paper documents in a secure physical location (a Physical Data Room) by uploading the document collection to a technologically secure website and permitting users to access the information remotely. When a company is up for sale they need to share a large document collection with potential buyers, and require a secure location to do so. Historically a room would have been set up by the seller's law firm and people from all over the world would fly into this location to review the documents. But this new technology made the process faster, cheaper and easier for all involved. The key to selling the system was to convince all parties involved that the integrity of their confidential documentation was maintained at all times.

The product was extremely interesting to me because it sat right on the cusp of the innovator/early adoption phase of the curve and, if it gripped, then its potential could be huge because these data rooms were built for every single company sale process globally. These sales processes, also known as M&A transactions, were plentiful despite the downturn and my research showed there were approximately 6,000 per year. I sought the opinion of a number of people in the industry and all agreed it was a good idea in principle, as long as the technology stood up.

At this point in time there were only two providers of this technology in the market, and both were US-based. One was a small, privately owned company that specialised in just this technology, and the other was a massive corporation that had begun to offer it as part of a wider product suite. Both had distinct benefits that appealed. The larger firm instinctively felt the better fit for a number of reasons. First, they were better positioned to approach the market as they had already gained the trust of their clients by supplying related services. Second, it was a circa $800-million company and so had the money to invest in new technologies should the opportunity prove worthwhile. Third, I was keen not to repeat the same mistake as before and get involved with a product that didn't have longevity. If I joined this firm and the technology didn't prove to be as successful as anticipated, then I could just work my way around their other products. All these advantages were echoed by my clients and this company felt perfectly positioned to dominate if they had the right sales team and leader.

The smaller firm, however, had all the appeal of a more flexible, specialist approach, which I had enjoyed in my previous role. They had a great website and well-conceived brand and I felt they could potentially offer me the autonomy to dominate and lead the product into market. I needed to understand more, so I decided the smartest approach was to set up an interview with the smaller of the two firms. My thinking was that, at a minimum, I would glean a lot of information from this interview, and that this firm had one final overriding attribute. Small technology companies that typically specialised in providing just one solution, but do it better than anybody else, are likely to be acquired at some point by bigger firms. If I could negotiate performance-based equity as part of my package, then it might be a great move. The worst-case scenario for considering the smaller firm first was that, if everything did not work out as expected, then it would be a great stepping-stone to jump to the competition. Approaching it this way round meant, as long as I established myself as the top salesman, it would be much easier for me to negotiate my salary up when moving to the competing firm. Based on this logic, I called the Sales Director of the smaller company and expressed my interest in working for them. He referred me to an agent who was handling their recruitment, so I contacted him and set up an interview.

I have come to know a number of superb recruitment agents over the years, but on the whole I have found a good majority of them under-qualified to make judgments on their candidates' abilities and career direction. As a result I generally loathe dealing with them, and wasn't particularly looking forward to my meeting. True to form this chap didn't fail to disappoint. He turned up late and opened our conversation by explaining he had taken a look at my CV and saying, "So tell me what makes you think you can opt out of the workforce for two years and then swan back into the industry and get a job?"

He clearly enjoyed flaunting his position as gatekeeper, but I refused to respond to his arrogance and answered his questions sincerely. I had to temper my natural instinct to attack him, and decided from the offset to treat him as a client. I shared my surprise at his response to my resume, because it demonstrated a level of success that few of my peers could put a claim to. He reminded me of two similar characters I had met when visiting numerous recruitment agencies between graduating and landing my first job. Both told me that my personality simply wasn't cut out for a career in sales.

After 20 minutes, he was getting really boring, so I decided to close it down and ask him what he had to lose by putting me forward. I offered to connect him to previous employers to get some comfort that my absence would not reflect adversely on my sales performance. He gave me a rant about how he worked for his client and not his candidates, but my favourite quote, which will always stay with me, was that he considered me "borderline unemployable" with so much time out of the industry, and that it went against his better judgment even to put me forward. I empathised with his position and massaged his ego, eventually of course getting his recommendation to the company direct. Leaving his cheap, day-rented office space I wondered how many decent salespeople he had crushed after the same treatment. The whole experience sat badly with me over the following few days, and I decided that, when I had re-established my status in the industry, I was going to revisit this.

Following two interviews with the company the job was mine, but there was little leverage to negotiate and, although the basic salary was lower than expected, the numbers balanced out on hitting target. Day one, I was expecting to hit the ground running, but was told not to contact clients until internally accredited to do so. This process of accreditation began with a week-long course in New York where I was made to recite a series of scripts and responses to client questions. From the offset they treated me, and their entire sales team, like idiots. Despite assuring them of my ability to articulate a pitch, the management insisted that I memorise the scripts, which were among some of the most awfully constructed and robotic ever written, or be penalised financially. It came down to poor leadership and it felt like being in a cult of some sort. My appeals not to sell a new product in this way fell on deaf ears. It took four weeks to get accredited and learn the scripts, in which time I hadn't called a single client. In addition, it was explained several weeks after joining that I would not be managing my previous accounts and contacts. This felt utterly pointless and I concluded that this company was not the environment for me.

My focus shifted to positioning myself in the best possible light before approaching the competition. I kept my head down, and a client friend mandated me on a couple of good-sized deals towards the end of my second month, which catapulted me to the top of the sales leader board. The deals were contested against the company I was about to approach, so I asked my friend to contact their management team and suggest that they hire me. This was my chance to exit, so I wanted my name to be bandied about prior to getting in touch.

It all happened around the same time as our monthly "compulsory" team building drinks. Everyone was a little drunk and I decided to share my confusion with the Sales Director as to why he used the recruitment agent that interviewed me before joining. After I had shared my experience, he told me that the rest of the team also echoed my sentiments. He was happy to divulge the agent's payment terms, which turned out to be a 90-day probation period for each hire before commission was paid. Everything had fallen perfectly into place. Unbeknown to my boss, I would be resigning shortly before the agent's probation period expired, so the time he had spent meeting with me was in fact a complete waste of his time. I felt losing his fee was a just outcome for his appalling behaviour.

The following week, I called a headhunter friend and asked her to make the introduction to the new company on my behalf. In turn she would receive a hefty fee for doing so, part of which she would share with me. She indicated that I was the top salesperson at the competing firm and the resulting meeting happened very quickly. That evening I had a beer with the International Head of Sales. We immediately developed a rapport and he has since become a lifelong friend. We discussed the spirit of his firm and how they treat their salespeople. This was of key importance, as I was not prepared to go through the same idiotic process of memorising scripts. He explained that his firm was the clear market leader in their core businesses and had the top salespeople in the industry, one of whom was earning over $1million per year. I had already heard enough. Within a week the contract was signed, which represented a 50% uplift on my basic salary to sell their new product release as well as a massive commission uplift – over triple my current potential on hitting the target. He agreed to give me back my old clients as well as the biggest potential accounts in the world.

I couldn't have imagined, or intended, that my employment at the first company would be so brief. It was entirely my fault for not better understanding the culture and company expectations prior to joining. In this instance, there was no harm done because a potential exit was part of my backup plan from the offset. However, I was keen to make this next move a permanent one, and things couldn't have worked out better under the circumstances. An important lesson had been learnt:

KEY MARKER #5

IS THE MANAGEMENT TEAM GEARED FOR SUCCESS?

Will the culture positively support what I need to achieve my targets, or negatively impact my ability to earn?

The new company was everything the other was not. I had free reign in Europe and knew this was my opportunity to dominate in a new industry.

The global market for my product had been independently valued at $500million, and it was explained to me from the very beginning that my business division was being built for eventual sale which, all things being equal, would take three to five years to achieve. The financial year ran February 1st to January 31st, and I started at the end of August. This meant a five-month run up to prepare for my first full earning year. As lead-time from deal announcement to execution was often a matter of days, I would have to work hard and fast to get word to potential clients. This was transactional sales rather than consultative, and fairly new to me. Deals were mainly won on a single meeting and the very short sales cycle required a razor-sharp sales pitch as well as technical sales skills in order close quickly.

This fitted my personality perfectly. There was little to distinguish our product features from the main competitor, but the most potent advantage we had was existing relationships with the key players on the majority of these M&A deals. This meant that my job was as much about leveraging existing client relationships as building new ones. The only glitch was that my commission was paid on an annual basis, three month in arrears. This meant that commission on a deal signed in early February would not be paid for approximately 15 months – i.e. end of April the following year. This sat uncomfortably with me, but I convinced myself it would be a good savings plan. My personal goal was to pay off my mortgage in the next 12 months and replenish a chunk of the equity blown on my travels.

My job became an obsession and my revenues were unprecedented. It was not unheard of for me to pitch in three different countries in a single day. It was a sales massacre in part due to our existing relationship network, but also because I knew the weak, robotic pitch of our only competitor and so was able to position myself favourably and prepare for every eventuality. I devised a damning presentation, which gently undermined any unique selling points they claimed to possess. In total honesty, my aim was to prove that their scripted sales pitch was utterly ineffectual and that furthermore, if they had listened to my genuine grievances, they would still have all the skills I could bring to the table. Life was great, the business was flying, I loved my job and at the end of my first full year of selling had racked up a bonus that surpassed all my expectations. I was due my first commission payment since starting 18 months before.

On the day it was due, the company informed me that it had been decided they would only pay a fraction of the bonus that had been agreed. The outcome, that followed several months of infighting and uncertainty, was that I did receive the majority of the bonus, but my commission plan was altered to a system with no determinable metrics upon which to calculate my earnings. There was little choice other than to accept it or leave. I loved my job, so I stuck it out for another year, only to receive less than 50% of the commission in my original agreement. Regrettably, it was time to go, having collected two more concrete key markers that were prerequisite to any future position I would consider:

KEY MARKER #6

THE IMPORTANCE OF A CLEAR AND DEFINED COMMISSION PLAN.

Never again would I agree to being paid 15 months in arrears or accept a compensation structure that did not state a direct and quantified reward for my personal contribution. The only reason I can ever imagine a company not offering a clear payment structure is if they wanted to alter the terms later.

KEY MARKER #7

THE IMPORTANCE OF A CLEAR AND DEFINED REPORTING STRUCTURE.

During this tenure I had two bosses and a "dotted line" to another. It was a calamity, which led to infighting and uncertainty on my behalf. Whenever I won a large mandate they were all clambering to claim credit and yet when I wanted something done they seemed to disappear and blame each other. It took so much of my time and energy I would never again agree to work within such a disjointed reporting system.

It was easy for me to make a move because I had been approached by several competing companies with new products, as well as my ex-employer on a number of occasions with the promise that there would be no scripts to recite. So, I made my discontent known within the industry and was quickly approached by a small European-based corporate whose core business was in the same space as my current employer. I knew a little of this company from pitching against them; they had been on my radar for a while as a viable player in the industry. My clients spoke highly of them and were supportive of a potential move. The sentiment at the time was that they had a good product and were pleasant to deal with, but lacked the senior-level relationships to do any real damage in the market. It was a good match. I took several months and numerous meetings to be sure that joining this company was the right move. It was especially important not to make any mistakes because I was leaving a great job and at the top of my game.

The company was private equity owned, looking to strengthen their team and exit the market in the form of a trade sale within the next three to five years. Equity wasn't on the table, but I had negotiated a package that meant being able to close a lot less revenue and still be paid substantially more than at my current employer. I also negotiated to sell their entire product suite, which put them, and me, in direct competition with my current employer. A big part of the incentive to join was that this new company was working to release a full product upgrade that would establish them as having the most advanced technology of its kind in the market. Taking into account my contractual obligation not to join a competing company within 12 months of leaving my current role, this new product was scheduled for release just prior to my joining, and I would have full responsibility for its introduction to the market.

It felt correct moving to a smaller, more flexible operation and dealing with the same client base. A further incentive to move was the 12-month lock-out clause in my contract that appealed because I was a little burnt-out. This included six months on full pay from my previous employer, followed by a six-month non-compete clause, which I negotiated to be back-paid by my new employer. This gave me a year in which I was contractually unable to work in my industry, but still on full pay, so giving me plenty of time to recharge my batteries. In hindsight it was too long, but worth the wait to have an identical role as before with a clear commission plan and simple reporting structure. The only other significant observation worth mentioning, which I didn't pay any attention to at the time, was that my new company was infamous for having a high staff turnover. From my perspective, this wasn't relevant and I was assured that they would leave me to focus entirely on selling to my existing client base.

IT SOMETIMES PAYS TO LOSE

I didn't pay attention to the state of the markets until nine months into my contractual 12-month absence. By then, the recession had gripped and deal volumes were substantially reduced. The majority of my good contacts had, once again, been made redundant in my absence, and I started to become anxious as my start date approached. Working in an economic downtown was not new to me, but this time the spiral of decline seemed far worse, and accelerating week by week. A few alarms bells began to ring around this time. The goalposts were being moved with my new firm, and my account deck was changing from what had been agreed. My entertainment budgets had been cut to an unworkable level, yet I was still expected to maintain relationships with the biggest players in the market.

During my absence, many of my old customer support team had kept in touch and helped me stay up-to-date with what was happening in the market. It's a small world in the financial markets, and my ex-colleagues kept the link in case I was hiring in the future. One of them told me that my ex-boss was focused on obstructing my path back into the market. Apparently the sales teams had been instructed that, should they pitch against me on any deal, they should reduce their fee to zero so that I could never win a deal. Part of me liked this because it meant they were more interested in my demise than doing good business, a vulnerability I would be able to exploit when the time was right. In addition, the technology was maturing and a handful of other companies had developed similar products over the previous year, so each pitch was more heavily contested because there were more providers and fewer deals. I would have to bring my A-game to the table on every level.

During my first week back in the office, it was clear people were keen to see what I was going to do. If I am honest, I didn't really know. All I knew was that I didn't want to be predictable, so I had to suppress my natural instinct to attack every deal. The promised new technology release was still under development and so, pound for pound, I couldn't yet compete effectively against my old firm. I also knew my previous firm could not sustain a strategy that gave away every deal I pitched for free, so my plan was to pitch deals half-heartedly and over-price them with the aim of losing them. It broke my heart to do this, but there was a bigger picture.

These deals were small, and their intentional loss was aimed at getting my competition to lower their guard. Over the following weeks I made a point of feigning frustration to my old teammates, and this circulated around the industry as intended. My competitors became complacent, thinking that they could easily win against me, which gave me some breathing space until a big deal came around. In the meantime I had aligned myself with some junior salespeople in my team. I needed their contact base to source deals as mine had been decimated in the downturn. They started to feed me market information regarding which deals were coming up, and one stood out as an interesting opportunity.

Big deals in such a weak market were few and far between, but the story that circulated in the office was that there was a very large transaction about to begin with a FTSE 100 corporate and our company had been excluded from the pitch process. The Request for Pricing (RFP) document had been sent a week earlier to my ex-employer, as well as two other competing firms, and the person telling me this thought the deal had already been mandated. There were four parties involved in the decision-making process: two banks, one law firm and the corporate that would be paying the bill and who made the ultimate decision. All we had was the name of the point person who was coordinating the effort at one of the banks.

The sales team had already accepted defeat, but this was a big deal and instinctively it felt like the opportunity I had been waiting for. There was no time to procrastinate – the first step was to contact the person running the quote-gathering process, verify the validity of my information and at least get included in the process.

I made the call to the guy who was working for one of the two investment banks and, despite having never spoken to him before, managed to convince him to include us in the pitch process. He explained that the quote process had already been running a week and that the quotes would be reviewed and a decision reached that evening. I had until close of business that day to submit my detailed pricing specification and be considered. It was approximately 1pm. He also confirmed that in addition to himself, there were three other people involved in the decision-making process, but to safeguard the confidential nature of the deal, he wasn't prepared to share their identities. This seriously diminished my chance of success, but regardless I still felt this was a golden opportunity. I had to move fast.

To stand any chance of pitching this effectively I needed more information, and asked him if we could have a quick coffee as I was in the area. Saying that I was in the area was stretching it a bit, but experience has proven that it's always much easier to probe for information face-to-face. To my surprise he agreed, so I jumped in a taxi and began the 30-minute journey across London to their offices. To get him to open up a little I needed to appear more knowledgeable about the transaction. Whilst in transit I had one of my junior sales reps do some research into the potential identity of this client. It is often possible to glean this from historical deal data and online industry-specific rumour mills. We quickly devised a shortlist of two potential candidates, with one company standing out as a frontrunner. I could discreetly convey this information over our coffee in the hope that he would go some way to confirm its validity.

From the offset I could tell the quote coordinator was doubtful of my success, which made me think that either the deal had already been mandated or that he had a pre-existing relationship with another supplier. Regardless, confident that we were both talking about the same deal, I explained that I knew the corporate identity and had worked with them in a previous role – a slight exaggeration in that I had heard of them but had never spoken to them – and was aware that they liked to use their long-standing corporate advisers. He responded by saying he couldn't confirm the validity of my information, but that if we were both talking about the same transaction then my assumptions *might* be correct. His smile, tone and body language all affirmed my suspicions. Now I needed the internal project name, which is an alias given to the transaction to safeguard the identity of all involved. It turned out to be Project Tango.

The code name was vital in opening conversations with the other people involved, as it showed we were talking about the same deal. Finally, now that we were on the same page, I suggested that for a job of this size I would expect to quote in the region of £50,000 for our services, and asked if this sounded reasonable based on the quotes he had already received. He didn't confirm, but suggested that were I to submit a price in that region for this particular transaction, I would be at the lower end of the quotes he had received. Now I knew the price point that everyone was quoting and could position my price exactly where I wanted it to be. I had a colleague type up a formal proposal while continuing to chase down the other decision-makers.

The meeting of decision-makers to award the mandate was imminent and I still had to connect with three other parties. Their identities were now clear, but cold calling was the last possible option and almost certainly suicide considering their seniority. In need of an angle, I put a call into an associate friend of mine at a law firm and asked his advice. He said it was a tall ask to leverage his network, but he had once played cricket with a guy who worked for the legal partner in question. The person I was trying to reach just happened to be one of the most respected and senior corporate lawyers in the industry. My friend put me in touch with an associate who worked for him and I shared my predicament. He explained they were all extremely busy at the moment working on Project Tango, but from where he was sitting he could see the senior partner working in his office and would briefly introduce me before transferring over. From that point, it was up to me.

I was patched through and explained that I was pitching on the upcoming mandate for Project Tango and would be in the building in 10 minutes. If he had time, I would appreciate a very short meeting to introduce myself and explain why our services were perfectly positioned to execute this transaction on their behalf. He agreed, but this too was a complete fabrication because I was nowhere near the office, so I hastily grabbed my coat and flew over there in a taxi. He met me in the lobby and gave me ten minutes as promised. He had the air of authority that you only get from the most senior players in the industry, so I cut straight to the chase. He was appreciative of my efforts to ascertain his position on the deal as well as the time to visit and express our commitment to the process. I asked if he had any preference for provider and he said he didn't, so I asked for his support and he told me that this meeting had not hurt my cause. I asked him who else in his firm would be involved and he said that further meetings were unnecessary and that I had already covered it. Turns out he was the most senior influential party in the process outside of the corporate who would be paying the bill, and I knew they probably would not go against his recommendation. Nobody else pitching for this deal had managed to get in front of this guy, and the balance was starting to fall in my favour. I had inserted myself into a massive process at the final hour and contacted half of the decision-makers. It wasn't over yet, though, as the second banker, as well as the ultimate decision-maker at the corporate, were still to be convinced.

As I left the lobby, I put a call in to the third decision-maker on the deal at a different bank, explaining my recent meeting with the senior partner at the law firm and that he had suggested I get in touch. Dropping his name led to a frank and open conversation, and 20 minutes later I was having coffee with the banker. He was the most neutral of the four and didn't mind working with us or our competition, so the final and most important person to convince was the corporate who would be paying the bill. I had a suspicion that this banker might have been pacifying me and may already have had a preference for another provider, but I felt comfortable that he was the least vocal of the four deciding parties, so I wasn't bothered. In the meantime my colleague sent our quote in with numbers that positioned us second from the bottom of the four submitted proposals. What tended to happen in this industry was the top and bottom quotes were dismissed from the offset, and then a second round process began between the short-listed firms.

It was now 6.30pm on a dark and wet winter evening. Sitting in my office and feeling tired, I put in a number of calls to the Head of Legal Services at the corporate who was coordinating the effort on their behalf. There was a chance she would still be at her desk as they often work all hours when a large deal is on the table. It had been a manic day but I didn't want to go home without having spoken to the corporate, so I headed for dinner around the corner from my office to take stock. The decision was imminent and it was essential to reach the final decision-maker and convince her that I was the man for the job. I called several times that evening but only managed to reach voicemail, and opted not to leave a message. It was 9.30pm and the office was now completely empty. I decided to make one last call, and was taken by surprise at how quickly she answered. With no time to think, I immediately kicked into gear and wasted no time in explaining who I was, who I knew and my position in pitching for their work. She explained they were all too busy that evening to select a provider and that the decision had been postponed until lunchtime the next day. I managed to convince her to have a very brief breakfast meeting at 8am the following morning. We met and she generously gave me the opportunity to deliver a very concise and sincere pitch, convincing her that, although we were the smallest company in the pitch process, we were the best for the job. Early that afternoon she called me to award my firm this hugely important mandate.

This deal generated well over £1million for my company and was the highest grossing, highest margin deal of the year. That, by itself, allowed me to surpass my first-year annual target. I had been at the company for approximately three months and against all odds had re-established my status in a tough market. The deal was also a perfect springboard to network out in the industry and build new senior-level contacts. Some months down the line I visited the corporate and asked the Head of Legal out of interest why they chose to work with us. She said the two banks were neutral, the senior legal adviser had found me highly professional when we met and that she personally had never seen anyone so keen to work with her. She thought anybody that keen would certainly do a good job, and so she chose me.

A few months later I bumped into a guy from the competition. He was a strong sales rep and we knew each other by reputation. I heard him shout over a long bar, "Oi, I want a word with you, Bartlett! That was you on Project Tango, wasn't it?" He shook my hand and told me that the bankers in the process had told him, off the record, that his firm had been awarded the mandate for Project Tango. As a result he had already booked the business back at the office. It wasn't until he was at a family barbecue over the weekend that the call came in from the coordinating banker telling him that the deal had gone elsewhere. He said he couldn't believe it, but knew that it was me. I would like to say that I felt bad, but nothing gave me more pleasure than to teach him a lesson. He was a very experienced salesman but, on this occasion, he had made some cardinal errors during the pitch phase. He only communicated with the two banks that represented 50% of the deciding parties. In fact, he only covered the least important 50% in the process, and assumed the others were too senior to be bothered.

Despite my successes at this company, I never felt like I belonged. I was able to keep my head down and focus on sales, but I couldn't ignore the fact that the management had no idea how to take the company forward. The real problem with this business was that it was trying to evolve from being a manual service provider to a digital one, and the management, who had not changed for many years, had no idea how to do this. The new product release that was promised at this company a year prior to my joining still wasn't finished three years later, at which point the market had moved on. Furthermore they were squandering vast amounts of money building a different product without canvassing opinion or understanding the potential needs within the market. A consequence of their naivety was that the product was poorly received and took a nosedive shortly after launch. This impacted my budgets and the release of the product I needed to compete, which ultimately hit my pocket and led to the next compulsory prerequisite when considering an employer.

KEY MARKER #8

IS THERE AN ADEQUATE BUDGET TO DRIVE SUCCESS AND PRODUCT DEVELOPMENT?

This is an absolutely essential question, especially in a market that's moving quickly, because when a product takes off it isn't long until others join the party, so it is important to stay one step ahead at all times. It is also essential in a market driven by corporate entertaining to have an adequate budget to generate and maintain the necessary relationships with potential prospects and clients.

In addition to budgetary constraints and the mismanagement of funds, within the office there was a clear division between the attitude of the sales team and the customer support team who harboured a historical resentment dating from many years back. A consequence was that they communicated poorly with the sales team and made many mistakes when executing deals. The turnover of staff was high, which I knew before joining and chose to ignore, because new salespeople became quickly discontented with the lack of adequate leadership. The only other time I had seen such a high staff turnover was at the company who had required me to memorise scripts. Both companies were a lesson in how not to manage a sales team, and I came to realise that lack of employee retention is a clear indication that something is fundamentally wrong at the core of a company. In some cases it is possible to compensate for poor management with sales effort, but I am now very sensitive to this when considering new companies and products to sell.

KEY MARKER #9

IS THERE HIGH STAFF TURNOVER, AND IF SO, WHY?

This key marker is focused entirely on the management of the business. Do the senior board have the experience not only to drive the business forward, but also promote a winning and harmonious team spirit where all are working towards a common goal? High staff turnover suggests they don't, and it is important to assess, prior to joining, how this will impact my ability to hit my targets.

Salespeople notoriously like to share their success, especially when they are earning big numbers. Their product may already be well established but this isn't important because products can become hot at various times for any number of reasons. What is important is that if my alpha instincts detect that a legacy product has suddenly begun generating big numbers, but is being sold by a tired or complacent sales team, then I always like to look a little closer. There can be any number of reasons as to why a product suddenly hits a positive groove – for example, new legislation can exponentially increase the demand of certain compliance products as they become essential for businesses just to keep operating. Regardless of the reason, if I don't rate the salespeople or can see a gap in their technique, then I consider that this might be a golden opportunity because with focus, discipline and relentless application of The Basics, which follow, it is very easy to dominate such a team. Big money eventually brings the best salespeople – it's just a natural consequence of the industry. The key is to be the first on the scene and land grab as much as possible while the going is good.

KEY MARKER #10

IS THE SALES TEAM TIRED, LAZY OR COMPLACENT?

Where is the best place to hear about this? Normally at social gatherings or industry-related events, as salespeople brag about their success. I always make a point of asking which product is currently hot and who is making the most money.

CONCLUSION

I consider myself lucky to have worked for a vastly different group of employers during the first 15 years of my career. It has enabled me to gain a great deal of experience within different sales environments and formulate my own strategies for both sales as well as managerial success. The following summary of what I look for from a new product and employer will now have more context, and I will continue to build upon many of these points in the following chapters.

First and foremost, understanding the type of sales role that is best suited to my personality and skill set has been integral in allowing me to select companies and products to sell. I am a new business salesman who looks for products that are low on the adoption curve in order to take advantage of the early exponential rise in market acceptance. The curve also shows the correlation between price and relative market adoption. Towards the apex of the curve, as competitors flood the market, there is pressure on the ability to charge a premium and so the chargeable price falls when companies undercut one another as a tactic to enter or disrupt the market. This is another reason I like to sell new products – because I can take advantage of the associated higher charging potential that they offer and maximise my margins.

Next, I insist on a clear and defined commission structure that demonstrates a quantified path to achieving my personal financial goals. Ideally the product and company would have progression and my product would be one of a suite of products so, if my product reaches a point where it has saturated the market, I can move to sell the other products.

Following on from this, I have learnt the importance of working for a company with an adequate cash flow, and one that is prepared to commit sufficient funds to develop the product and support the sales team as it grows and diversifies. When considering technical products, another way to safeguard future earnings is to ensure that the product is continuously redeveloping and innovating, based on client requirements. If there are not adequate funds or a leadership structure that encourages this, then it doesn't necessarily mean it isn't a good job or product to sell, but it is likely to be a role without longevity. I want to be conscious of this from the offset, and plan accordingly.

It is important to understand how the company has calculated its predicted revenues and potential market size. Then, I do my own research and confirm that we agree. If it's a new product, then it is useful to know who has seen it to date, what they are expecting from my territory, and who else they are hiring. I speak to customers or potential customers to understand their view of the product or concept to date and its potential. Often overlooked is whether the market is ready to buy the product. Sometimes a new technology or concept can be so cutting-edge that clients are scared to commit their budgets to be the first adopters. It is easy to burn a lot of time and money as a first-mover trying to educate the market on the importance of your product.

If I am looking to sell something that is cutting edge or early in its development, then a good indicator of market perception is how many orders are pre-sold leading up to launch. Money talks, and if clients are prepared to commit prior to launch then it's a good sign that the company has built the product correctly and it meets the market requirements.

Culturally, I prefer to work for a new team, or hire one from scratch. In my experience, it is most productive to be surrounded by highly motivated peers who can deliver in their own assigned territories so that the product and company are viewed positively in their entirety. This is another reason I like to work with products low in adoption because it is easier to help define the culture by example from an early stage. Likewise, it is important to know whom you are working for; I want to understand my boss, their background and whether they are sub-par or exceptional. Do they have the experience to create a harmonious and productive sales environment, or are they stale and making it up on the fly?

Ultimately, the competence of my boss shouldn't drastically affect my ability to hit my goals, but it is useful to know to what degree I can rely on my reporting line and build this into my overall plan. Regardless, I want a clear reporting line and take heed of markers such as high staff turnover or little or no defined managerial strategy to market. It is more important that the *company* has a precedent of releasing successful products, as opposed to my bosses' experience, so I like to look carefully at who is setting the wider strategy from above. It is likely that, if this person is exceptional, then they will want to hire good people below them, so if my boss does prove to be sub-par, they won't last long. A good indicator of a company's, or an individual's ability to successfully deliver and manage a well-orchestrated product release is to look at the other products in their portfolio.

If the company specialises in one product and has aspirations to exit soon via a trade sale or IPO, then in the absence of performance-related equity I want to be extremely well compensated for my work for two reasons.

Firstly, I bring a lot of value to the company which will positively impact their sale multiple, and secondly, if a company does put itself on the block for sale then its future comes with a level of uncertainty and I want to be compensated for working with this knowledge. This can also be achieved by negotiating a golden parachute provision before joining. This clause in your employment agreement covers a range of benefits that apply in the event of a takeover, or should your employment be terminated through unforeseen circumstances. I grew tired of working all hours to make other people tons of money midway through my career so, ever since, I have always ensured that my contribution to the bigger picture is recognised, in one way or another, from the offset.

Everything written here is simply a wish list that is personal to me. It is entirely unrealistic to expect to have a politically free working environment with complete autonomy and unlimited budgetary restraints. Big money draws big personalities so it's always a balancing act. For me, the most successful and productive environments are those that align as many as possible of these key markers and big personalities to support my way of working, and this is best achieved by joining a company or product as early as possible to set the example. It's about recognising the good, neutralising the bad, understanding each other and aligning to a common goal that is nothing short of market dominance through excellence. For me, this runs in sync with my personal goals that are the foundation upon which I operate.

The ultimate opportunity to be clear about all of the aforementioned points is during the interview phase. An interview is not an opportunity to beg for a job; rather I view it as an open and sincere conversation to understand if there is a good fit between the organisation and myself. If not, then it isn't personal, but it saves time for all involved to be clear from the beginning. It is never a single meeting, but takes time to develop a relationship with the potential company and establish mutuality where all aspects of working together are agreed and understood. As far as possible I use the interview phase to remove the moving parts and quantify every aspect of the role. Doing all the groundwork prior to joining means you just have to get the product sold and the implementation, which is covered in the next section, is the easy bit.

Section 2

The Basics

Sales techniques can easily be learnt, but there comes a point when technique and personal style come together to define the overall character of a salesperson. This process tends to happen early in a career and, In my experience, the type of character that evolves changes little thereafter. This is largely because a salesperson and their associated success are defined primarily by their personality and the motivations that drive them.

For example, I have never witnessed an average salesperson who makes 30 to 50 out of a possible 80 phone calls a day suddenly decide to consistently double their efforts for no apparent reason. I have seen people temporarily ratchet up their game because they have an urgent need for more income given that they have recently married, have just became a parent or are at risk of losing their job. But, these are cases where the motivation is coming from an external stimulus, not an internal one. Top salespeople, on the other hand, are driven to maximise their productivity every minute of the day, not every random month or so when they feel like it.

My early career was heavily focused on being a technically better salesperson. As someone who responds best to being led by example, I always sought a mentor and the first substantive instance of this came in my second company. Before I joined, a number of people had already told me that my new boss was an exceptional salesperson, and I remember the feeling of inadequacy watching him conduct our first meeting together in front of clients. He made everyone in the room comfortable, was a superb listener and had a great clarity about his client's needs as well as the solution he offered. Furthermore, he executed a detailed and insightful sales process; yet it all felt like a very natural conversation. The follow-up points were concise, and key to the meeting's success was that he acknowledged every single buying signal and objection. In closing, the product was sold in a seemingly effortless fashion and we were all left with a positive feeling. It was a masterclass derived from years of experience.

Over the coming months, we spent many hours discussing our respective styles so I could understand how to improve. He explained that the one salesperson he most admired during his career had told him that the secret to sales success is simply to "be brilliant at The Basics". His feedback on my performance was that although my incredible run of sales success to date had put me ahead of my years in terms of experience, I had yet to truly internalise and believe in The Basics. They needed to flow naturally from me at every point of client contact, and understanding their value was essential to making the most of every opportunity.

Clearly this stuck, and throughout a diverse career of both observing other salespeople as well as reinventing my own style to suit vastly different sales environments, I can confidently state that there is a fundamental set of actions that I, and other top salespeople, do on a daily basis that others do not. This section is dedicated to my own interpretation of The Basics, and although their definition differs slightly from person to person, the core seems to hold true amongst the best in the industry.

The amazing thing about The Basics is that the vast majority of salespeople know them, some think they are above them, and others simply can't be bothered to do them. A former boss once told me, "You have the ability to cruise through the day and still do better than the average salesperson's best effort." Yes, because even if I am tired or hung-over or bored, or my brain feels like shutting down, I still perform this set of actions every day and on every deal. It simply baffles me how often salespeople conduct a meeting without asking a single question, vomit some product features across the table, offer a price, and then thank the client for their time and leave. This isn't selling, nor is it the actions of a person interested in selling. The Basics protect me from this behaviour and also stop me from believing my own hype. It's easy to gain sales success and sit back on your laurels, only to find a gap in your pipeline from losing focus or discipline.

This fundamental set of ten principles complements the prerequisite sales training, is the nucleus of my own personal success, and helps safeguard me against the many external influences that can obstruct my goals.

1. "A VISION WITHOUT A STRATEGY IS A DREAM..."

This quote has resonated with me ever since hearing it during an early sales course. The previous section explained that one of my fundamental markers for picking a product was that the earning potential must fit with my own personal financial goals. In support of this, I then work backwards to be clear where the product is in terms of demand and market adoption, confirm that my account territory can deliver these results and that my commission scheme fits. Everything is geared toward a final earnings figure, with each step quantified and formulated into a carefully conceived plan. This strategy keeps me motivated and on a defined path where all I have to do is execute.

An ex-colleague from early in my career was once giving his opinion of my sales results. He was in customer services and not sales, but we enjoyed a good relationship and he often joined my client meetings. During my absence, he apparently explained to the office that, "Lee can tell you on any given day and over any time frame what he is going to do, how he is going to do it and how much money he is going to make." He was right. As the market changes and the product moves through the adoption curve, I continuously evaluate and adapt my sales strategies to fit my end goal by working backwards over as many parameters as possible.

In addition to the company sales ledger, I maintain my own detailed personal sales records that include both invoiced items and payments received. My records include a number of models that chart my progress towards the target, and show my average monthly revenue in order to monitor seasonal trends and map my year accordingly. At any given time I can tell you how much has been invoiced and collected as well as predict with a degree of certainly what is coming in. Good Sales Directors should also be calculating this so that they can understand how the team is functioning and whether they are on course to hit the group targets. However, after working with some outrageously incompetent management, I keep my own tally for peace of mind. It is amazing how often my personal records did not tally with those of the company, and have saved me missing a commission cheque.

Another not so obvious element worth mentioning is that I always forward sell new product developments and counsel client feedback to confirm their intention to buy. This safeguards my future earnings and keeps my finger on the pulse with new products and features. As a result, I am able to adapt and become what the client wants throughout the entire process from pitch to sale and beyond. Good companies encourage and respond to this; not-so-good companies tend to be defensive and dismiss the feedback.

#1 IN SUMMARY...

I believe that focusing on your personal financial goals and reverse engineering a strategy at every level to achieve them is a basic and fundamental behaviour of a top salesperson. Most salespeople don't have a defined overall plan or see past the company revenue targets.

2. WORKING HARD AND SMART

Hard work, like success, is subjective, and if you ask a salesperson if they work hard, 99% of them will tell you they work harder than anyone they know. In my experience, though, the average salesperson works as if they are in a normal job, not one that rewards with performance-related pay. They swan in, make a few phone calls to hit their quotas, hide behind some admin because they "don't feel like it today", look for some positive affirmation from colleagues by discussing problem clients and reasons they didn't make a sale, remind everyone of their most successful deals or why someone got lucky with a big deal, book some meetings internally or externally, do some internet shopping and then go home at 5.30pm sharp. Within their psyche is an element of hope that things will be OK and the phone will ring with the odd bonus deal to keep them hitting their numbers.

Top salespeople don't do this, and they don't factor blind faith into their overall plan. They go to work for a reason – to get paid as much as possible. I realised very early on in my career that divine intervention wasn't something that can be relied on to make my calls or close my deals. The only way to guarantee success is to do the work, and making a sale is only possible if you are talking to a prospect. My strategy for negating hope from my sales results is to quantify what I expect to achieve from a working day.

So let me define my understanding of working hard. Working hard to me means doing the maximum possible *revenue generating* activities in a day while staying realistic. In the last chapter you will remember in my first role this turned out to be 80 calls a day, taking three short breaks and staying an hour later than required each day. The average was 50 calls per person per day. In my next and subsequent field-sales roles this was at least four face-to-face client pitches per day, plus two to three hours to complete my administration, follow up on action points and book subsequent meetings. Later in my career, with additional support from my secretary, I could effectively pitch six times a day because my support team freed up my non-revenue generating sales-related activities. This represents a full schedule that forces you to plan ahead a week or two in advance. To stand any chance of achieving this, it's important to stay focused and not get dragged into external distractions such as office politics or banter.

In addition to meeting volumes, it was part of my strategy always to contact five new prospects a day. Not a huge number, and only one hour of work, but essential to maintain momentum. It is impossible to handle this volume of work without being well organised, and so I strove to work efficiently by scheduling follow-up appointments immediately after every meeting and completing non-client facing administration, such as proposal documents, whilst travelling or at home.

My response to a sales-related plateau has always been the same – to remind myself that you can't make a sale unless you are talking to a prospect. Just hit the phone and create an opportunity. Rejection is part of the profession, so I would devise strategies to help me to overcome any lack of result. If, for example, three separate prospects in a row had declined to meet, I would work no matter how late until the next prospect agreed. Intrinsically linked to hope, rejection and working smart, is being disciplined enough to not waste time on people who don't make buying decisions or are non-committal. It is far better to see a situation for what it is and lose early than to waste time on an uninterested buyer in the hope that they may change. For me, selling is about doing good business. If you are dealing with a prospect who cannot see the potential and who doesn't like to say "no" until cornered, then it is best to call them out early and move on.

The fact is, on any given day, a higher proportion of my time is spent performing revenue-generating activities than any of my colleagues. I create a situation where there simply isn't time to procrastinate and nobody puts more pressure on me to perform than myself.

IN SUMMARY... #2

Placing a great value on time, working efficiently and to the maximum (quantified) potential in any given time frame, and not being distracted from revenue-generating activities are basic and fundamental behaviours of a top salesperson. Most salespeople don't do it.

3. BECOMING PUNCH DRUNK ON THE PHONE

Top salespeople are fearless when it comes to contacting prospects because they know they have something of value to offer. Whether calling the CEO of a major corporate or the buyer of a magazine subscription the tone, pitch and the message is always clear and well-received. One of my ex-bosses once said to me, "You can build better relationships on the phone than most can face-to-face," and this is all down to how I learnt to do it.

However, this wasn't always the case. In the beginning, the idea of making a call would leave me feeling intimidated and wanting to run away and hide. It took me time to understand how to iron out the kinks and develop my own confidence and style. Many salespeople never conquer this fear and an awful lot are *sales call reluctant*, taking every opportunity not to make an important call in case they mess it up or get a bad reception. This reluctance is often observed in salespeople trying to be New Business Salespeople, but who are better suited to Account Management. They are trying to conform to the former role because it is typically better paid, but the reality is they are in the wrong job and every day is spent out of their comfort zone. Other characters and reasons I have observed for call reluctance are:

Analysis paralysis: these master procrastinators over-analyse every aspect of making a call and compile endless notes to compensate for not executing. This is the reason I do not write scripts before a call.

Lack of goal: with no personal goal and a loose management structure these salespeople can blag their way through each day and get by with the bare minimum.

Poor proposition: these salespeople feel ashamed and are afraid to call someone because they don't have the conviction that their product or service will add value to the prospect.

Personal insecurity: the salesperson is more focused on their own inadequacies than communicating a valuable message to their prospect. They don't have a mechanism to process rejection any other way than personally.

There can be elements of each in the same person, but let me explain how I cured my own reluctance by taking the *decision* to make phone calls away from myself. I set a goal that meant speaking to (not simply calling, because they might not be in) a new person every five minutes. This fitted with my 80 calls a day and made it irrelevant who was listening to me. I began with scripts of my pitch, but panicked when taken off keel, so I moved on to trying to internalise the question, *What message do I want to convey, and how can I do that in less than 10 seconds?* It was simple: I have a product that is very relevant to your work; do you mind if I tell you a bit about it? Once comfortable and relaxed, I was off, making countless mistakes but learning much about myself. People told me to proverbially go away, and some memories make me cringe even now, but 80 calls a day for six months is over 10,000 calls. The cure to sales call reluctance, in my opinion, is volume, and the learning time of this skill can be compressed by simply making more calls.

Believe me, after 10,000 phone calls you will have developed the confidence to call any prospect - whatever their seniority. Your voice will not quiver and your pulse will remain at a steady 60 beats per minute. In my opinion, telesales is the very best introduction to a career in sales because it offers the opportunity to apply the techniques learnt on basic sales courses all day, every day. Mastering the phone rapidly develops the ability to circumvent gatekeepers, deliver a concise pitch in seconds, read buying signals and implement closing techniques – all from just the tone of the person's voice. Most importantly, I believe that this type of training helps you learn to master time. When nervous and unsure of the message you wish to convey, then everything is rushed from your speech to your thoughts. Taking control of time allows you to talk to a prospect just as you would with someone familiar. A normal, relaxed conversation has a natural tempo with pauses and breaks where each takes time to consider what has been said, as well as the direction in which to continue. Becoming punch drunk on the phone removes the anxiety associated with filling these breaks and empowers you to relax and focus solely on communicating an important message.

A good example was during my first telesales role while trying to develop a basic sales style as well as process my own fears about being rejected. I took the *decision* to change from using a script to speaking from the heart, and felt a little apprehensive. The name of the person to be called was Meredith Osborne, and we had never spoken. She answered the phone with a very posh and drawn-out thick South African accent, to which I replied:

"Hello Meredith, this is Lee Bartlett and I'm calling from..." I didn't even have the chance to say my company name when she interjected in an insistent tone:
"To whom am I speaking?" It caught me by surprise, and I quickly answered:
"Oh, my name is Lee Bartlett and I am calling from..." Again, she cut me short, and asked:
"Have we met?" A bit confused, I replied:
"Actually no, I don't think we have, but I would like..." Cutting me dead again, she insisted:
"Then you will address me as Ms. (pronounced Muzz) Osborne."

I couldn't believe how ridiculous she sounded, but after a couple of seconds, I realised that her request was fair enough. Apologising for being over-familiar, I continued to explain the purpose of my call and asked if she wouldn't mind considering my product. The penny had dropped: it was clear that, by simply speaking to people like human beings, there was no need to rush or fluster. It was a ground-breaking moment, and Muzz Oarzzborne became one of my favourite clients, having subsequently subscribed to my product. She was clear from the offset about what was acceptable to her and how she wanted the process to be conducted. A few weeks earlier, my response would have been very different and met with panic.

For me, it was important to embrace rejection as a natural part of my role. There are times when I might catch people at a bad time, execute a poor pitch or just be talking to someone who has no interest in my product, and that is fine. As long as my message is communicated in a sincere and professional manner, then the prospect can respond as they choose. The skill is to strive constantly to increase the conversion ratio from first contact to sale, and there are two ways to do this. First, make the same number of calls and get better, or second, keep your conversion rate the same and make more calls. Top salespeople monitor and work to improve both.

Pure New Business Salespeople like myself thrive on calling new prospects as well as pitching and closing deals on the phone. It's just a way of casting the net wider and achieving more in a day. There are three other things that have substantially increased my success on the phone.

Firstly, when selling a new product, I always refine my pitch on small accounts and less important prospects. This ensures that larger opportunities aren't sabotaged by an overzealous and naive approach.

Secondly, I always try not to ask someone for something, such as a meeting, without giving something in return as leverage. A common type of cold call in a previous role after a short introduction was, "Can I buy you a coffee and tell you a bit about my company?" The sentiment is quite low key and suggests someone with a level of seniority, but it was too easy to reject. Consider that the clients were busy corporate bankers who really don't need a stranger to buy them a coffee and, if the mood swung against them, it was often declined or postponed indefinitely. The actual suggestion of coffee or a formal meeting is fine, but it shouldn't be the focal point of the meeting request. Far better to preface it with a legitimate business reason and, if possible, a deadline, so you can book the meeting into the earliest available slot.

Third and finally, my phone is always switched on and gets answered, unless I am in a meeting or sleeping. Always being available and responding promptly to clients, especially out of hours, has helped me build impenetrable relationships over the years and is one of the most important aspects of my success. I have witnessed many salespeople lose deals because they are not contactable after 6pm and I, for one, will never be one of them.

#3 IN SUMMARY...

Thriving on contacting potential new clients by telephone, regardless of status, and maximising the ratio of first contact to sale are basic and fundamental behaviours of a top salesperson. Most salespeople are intimidated by the process or fail to do it effectively, even at a senior level.

4. PRODUCT EVALUATION AND PITCH PREPARATION

Whether the window of opportunity is 10 seconds or an hour, it is essential to be able to effectively pitch your product in any scenario. To cover every eventuality, I compile and internalise four pitches that are described below, but before beginning to do so, I consider two factors that help to maximise their impact.

I place great importance on my first impressions of the product and make detailed notes in anticipation of negative feedback. This is an essential process, especially for new products, and it helps to devise a more effective pitch by neutralising potential objections from the offset. An example is a product that struck me as looking remarkably like Microsoft Outlook. It felt a little outdated but could not be easily changed, so in anticipation of similar feedback from prospects, I turned it into a Unique Selling Point (USP) by saying, "We intentionally designed the product to resemble Microsoft Outlook because we wanted to create an interface with a familiar look and feel." This became useful again towards the end of the pitch when discussing customer support, as I could point out that the familiar design was intuitive enough to navigate without the need for additional training.

Next, in order to understand the type of pitch your prospect will expect, it is important to note where the product lies on the Product Adoption Curve. Selling is not a static process and your message evolves with market acceptance. In the early stages of product evolution, the pitch is more focused on convincing prospects that what you are offering is the future. Then, as it becomes accepted into a wider audience, the need to sell a concept disappears and it becomes more about what differentiates your product from the various alternatives. Paying close attention to this allows you to compile a presentation that supports the current level of understanding, anticipates objections and communicates your points in the most effective way.

The process of devising my four pitches begins with a one- or two-sentence "elevator pitch". This typically contains something credible about the company and serves to pique an interest that naturally draws the conversation into a preconceived direction. For example, when selling Virtual Data Rooms, if someone asked me about my work, my response would be something like:

"I work for a company that has recently developed a new technology called a Virtual Data Room, that is completely changing how some of the largest financial transactions are executed..."

Next, if they were not connected to the industry, I would add, "by allowing big companies that are up for sale to more effectively communicate with potential buyers anywhere in the world and ultimately make them a lot more money in the process."

However, if the person happened to be involved in any way with the process, a more appropriate next sentence would be, "by cutting transaction times, achieving a higher sale price, saving the bankers and lawyers involved hundreds of hours of administration, and costing a fraction of the price of the current way of doing it."

Depending on which of the various statements the prospect connected with, a common next question was, "How do you go about finding buyers worldwide?" I like this response because it shows that the person is interested in the process and trying to think it through. If the person is connected in any way to the administration of the process, the most important hook is all the time that they will not need to spend in the office by using my revolutionary technology. They instantly want to be my friend. Everyone wants to know about new things that are making a lot of money, so I was often asked how the technology was able maximise transaction value. And finally, a Corporate Director who was divesting their company would always take a strong interest in a product that streamlines the process, costs less and adds several millions to the sale price.

Having established an interest and addressed their questions with straight and concise answers, I explain the value of my product in more detail, emphasising the key features by subtly animating my body language and the inflection of my voice. For a free audio download of this pitch, please visit the resources section of www. leebartlettbestseller.com

"In principle it is really simple. We have invested a lot of money into developing what is essentially a *glorified electronic filing cabinet*, but what is special about the cabinet is that it's enveloped by a platform of *very sophisticated security*, and this guarantees that *only invited parties* can gain access to the confidential documentation that lies within. For example, if a large corporation is up for sale, then the technology allows potential buyers to simultaneously perform their due diligence whilst *remaining completely anonymous* from one another. The seller is then able to assess interest levels by *viewing the activity of each potential buyer* within the data room, and *what is unique about our system* is that we possess the most advanced set of tools to monitor the entire process and shortlist candidates. As the process of document review occurs in tandem, the time taken to complete the deal is *dramatically compressed* in comparison to the traditional way of doing it, and the *cost savings are substantial* – typically *around 10%* of the traditional process – so it's a *no brainer* for all involved. It is fair to say that *my team currently hosts the vast majority of the transactions* in the market and is the trusted partner to all the top-tier institutions. We recently completed (largest current deal) and uptake is increasing exponentially."

This entire description has been precisely constructed, and my verbiage is carefully chosen to ensure that the prospects don't feel overtly sold to. I consciously refrain from statements such as "we are the market leader", and use more amiable language to make the same point. The value proposition is legitimised by the assumptive-close that immediately follows the product features – explaining that the benefits of our system are supported by the fact that our clients view it as a no brainer. At this point, if I felt that my message had already been received, then I would omit the final two sentences so as not to labour the point. This short description left the prospect feeling that this is a revolutionary product that they need to know more about. Having established credibility, it is now my turn to ask some questions to establish their potential needs before continuing to execute a tight sales process.

The second of my preconceived presentations is a formal five- to 10-minute pitch that digs a little deeper into the USPs of my offering. It is very useful over a lunch meeting where a client has bought a colleague who knows nothing about my product, or also in formal meetings where the prospects are difficult and they want you to understand that they are in control. These latter characters like to insist that they are smart enough to understand immediately the deepest connotations of anything you say, and just want to skim the important points without offering up any information themselves.

Regardless of who is in attendance, or the time frame available to communicate my message, my pitches are always devised to empower the prospect to conduct the conversation however they choose. In this way they are always in control and are encouraged to drop their guard, while my subtly provocative statements seek to cast a wide net and pinpoint the important requirements upon which to drill down. As each of the points in my pitch are seamlessly interlinked, I can naturally maintain a well-executed sales process, even if the prospect takes the conversation off on an entirely different tangent.

In short pitch scenarios with an uncertain time frame in which to convey my message, interpreting body language is important in discovering the source of my prospect's professional pain. A nod of the head or a smile when describing the various features of my product is enough to suggest I have struck a nerve so, to be sure, I backtrack and confirm my suspicions. After identifying all the challenges they face, I re-address each of them, raise the value of my solution and pre-close whatever is on the table.

My third presentation is a full 20-minute formal presentation that fills in all the gaps of my shorter deck. This is perfect for boardroom pitches with small groups of specialist people, all of whom contribute to the decision-making process. Having attended literally hundreds of these pitches, it is my belief that you only have their attention for a maximum of one hour. This is dramatically reduced in beauty-parade type situations where you are being compared back to back with your competitors. On first entering the room I try to assess the *actual* pitch window rather than the allotted time frame.

Coming later in the parade often means that prospects are getting exhausted by sales drivel, and a telltale sign of this is the look on their faces. It is important to be flexible and have the necessary skill-set to conduct the meeting in any order that is required. Sometimes there is a fixed agenda, but other times they will just want you to get on with it. Proceeding in the format of their choice, I cut to the chase and if they want me to run with it, suggest a short 10-minute overview to introduce the company, product and features – in other words cast the net wide – then directly address their exact needs and areas they want to discuss. The ten-minute overview is an intentional underestimation and runs closer to 20 minutes, but suggesting a shorter time frame focuses their attention because everybody will be thinking, "It's just ten minutes." This provides a better framework upon which to draw them in and build rapport.

A successful meeting has to be mutually beneficial and merely dumping information and then leaving doesn't achieve this. In an hour slot, if my real window of opportunity is only 45 minutes, then a good ratio to aim for is: 20 minute presentation, five minutes from me for sales discovery related questions, and 20 minutes plus to discuss client specific questions and objections. This way, more than 50% of the meeting is a two-way discussion understanding how our businesses potentially fit together.

Finally, my fourth presentation is geared towards more formal public presentations with many people in attendance. This pitch is a slight adaption of my 20-minute deck that focuses on a small number of unique selling points. Talking to large groups is mainly a marketing exercise and, from experience, people don't typically retain a lot of information. It is better to leave participants with a short, concise message than an overwhelming collection of features.

The underlying motivation behind preparing these four approaches is to be able to pitch alone under any circumstances. This means identifying the level of detail required to answer business-critical questions without the need for a product specialist in attendance. Clearly there is a limit to what should be learnt; for example, selling a technical online system does not require me to know how every line of code is written, but aside from it being my job to pitch the product effectively, having a specialist join every meeting is not a practical use of internal resources to compensate for an inadequate understanding of the product. In addition, these experts are not typically savvy with the sales process and often say something counterproductive. For this reason, in my

THE NO.1 BEST SELLER

experience, it is far easier to build rapport with prospects and run a tight sales process entirely by myself.

My view of the appropriate use of product specialists is discussed later in Invisible Revenue, but it is never a point of confusion as to whether they should attend – you just ask your prospect the level of detail they require prior to the meeting and, if caught unaware, it is entirely reasonable to just take notes and respond after the event.

This level of preparation has always set me apart from my competition. I used to love it when my competition would turn up to a pitch en masse with their sales manager, product specialist, customer service representative, relationship manager or someone loosely connected to the deal. Why not bring your mum and dad too who can vouch for what a nice person you are? By contrast I always felt in a position of strength being ready for anything. It is sometimes argued that bringing in a large team shows commitment to the deal, but my track record of winning deals in this particular industry suggests that my clients don't agree. A short but related story:

It is protocol for a buyer to keep participating companies separate from one another prior to a competitive pitch. On this particular occasion it wasn't possible to segregate us, and we could all see one another in the reception room while waiting our turn. These scenarios were a great opportunity to unnerve rival firms before they entered the boardroom. Sometimes I would be friendly to the competing salespeople, and at other times totally ignore them, laugh at them or just shake my head. It would be subtle but the aim was to force an emotional pitch that was more focused on beating me than on the job in hand. On this particular occasion I was the first to pitch of the three potential suppliers, and by the time my presentation had finished I instinctively knew the mandate was mine. As I was being escorted through the reception toward the lift, three members of a competitive firm were heading to the room for their turn, so I stopped and shook hands with one of them. It was a brief interaction and, as the lead salesperson went to proceed, I held his gaze and mouthed, "It's too late." It was a bit of a joke and just felt like the right thing to do, but he was ab-so-lu-te-ly mortified. His colleagues were equally disgusted, and it made me laugh all the way back to the office.

About three hours later, he called my office and was furious with me. He explained that my unprofessional behaviour was appalling and had a detrimental impact on his ability to pitch because he could barely get his words out. It was difficult to empathise with him because my split-second comment had resulted in exactly the intended impact. This was a big deal that he would not have hesitated to win given half a chance. It made me wonder how I would have felt if the roles had been reversed. In total honesty, I doubt I would have even noticed because my focus is always firmly set on my prospect, what they need to get their job done, and what I need to do to book the business. Everybody else is irrelevant.

When it comes to pitching, I have been dropped into countless unforeseen situations and expected to cope; from a colleague dumping me in a room of 250 people with zero notice, to expecting a quick ten-minute coffee pitch to two people but actually being escorted into a boardroom for a formal pitch to 25 people all talking over one another. The fact is I absolutely love these scenarios, and it's fair to say that I have always had a reputation in my industry for being the best guy for the job. It is my rigorous preparation, understanding and mastery of presentation flow as well as a combination of all The Basics that ensures that I stay calm and make the most of every opportunity.

IN SUMMARY... #4

The ability to pitch your product effectively under any circumstances from a single sentence to an hour-long presentation while executing a defined sales process is a basic and fundamental behaviour of a top salesperson. Most salespeople don't do it well enough, even at a senior level.

5. SPEAKING AND LISTENING TO PEOPLE

Salespeople have a habit of intentionally overcomplicating what they say. It may be an attempt to sound more intelligent, but I am not sure they have thought it through. When we enter a store to buy something, the last thing we want is for the process to be confused by unnecessary jargon. Rather, we all appreciate straight-talking sales professionals who speak to us in a language that is tailored to our level of understanding.

There is a saying that "people buy people", and this tends to hold true as long as the products on offer are comparable in that they meet the buyers' needs. The ability to build rapport by communicating effectively with a prospect, to a larger degree, explains why a superior salesperson can often sell an inferior product. There have been many occasions when my product has been indistinguishable in terms of features, but the fact that I was running the process gave the client comfort that they were purchasing a better overall package. Throughout the pitch, the people awarding the mandate had chosen the package that made them feel the most comfortable and had come to see me as an equal and trusted part of their team, because we all spoke the same language.

To ensure my message has the maximum impact, I like to replace technical jargon with simple analogies in the form of short sound bites that are completely unrelated to my product. These sound bites conjure up a unique and unforgettable visual image in the mind of the prospect that is more easily remembered than a string of features.

More often than not, my analogies are USPs that are very difficult for the competition to dismiss. To give you an example, in the early days of selling Virtual Data Rooms I would ask prospects to imagine their "documents organised in a large filing cabinet floating amongst the clouds in a bright blue sky. The cabinet has a very large secure lock on it and a camera above the door so you can see who opens it". I would look and point up while imagining it myself. This description was useful when technologically illiterate company directors and in-house lawyers needed convincing of the basic concept behind the product on offer. It was a far more colourful image than the actual product and it gave everybody a framework upon which to be able to ask the necessary business critical questions. I could then connect the analogy to the features on a screen and answer their questions with live examples.

Building upon the initial concept, I would go on to describe that the way documents get uploaded to the filing cabinet is through a secure pipe plugged into the back of the cabinet, and explain that what set our technology apart from anybody else's in the market was that not only was our pipe the biggest, but the lock on our filing cabinet was the most secure in the industry. In fact it was as secure as was technologically possible so they could take comfort that we were safeguarding their confidential documents with the highest security protocols.

Even though my competition had devised a pitch that skipped over this information, the client was now very likely to ask them for a full specification of their system. I would be only too happy to draw a comparison that pointed out why we had gone that extra mile to protect the integrity of their proprietary document collection. It's much better than saying "Trust me, the system is really secure and much better than our competition," which I once heard a salesperson say as their only reference to the most vital question in the industry. I didn't know whether to laugh or cry, and no, it wasn't a genius assumptive selling technique. Furthermore, unless directly asked to compare, I would never mention my competition in a presentation, in the main because I didn't feel there was any.

It has always been an important part of my process to understand the sales pitch of competing companies and how to counter their comments effectively. If a prospect mentions a typical objection from my competition, then I am clearly second to the pitch, but I don't confront them with this knowledge as it would run the risk of spiking their egos. I just make the subtle adjustment in my own pitch to gently undermine what they have heard and be clear that my product is the better choice.

Throughout my early sales training, one of the most

commonly discussed topics was "asking open questions". It was tediously repackaged and I could never understand why it was such a revelation because, if you are interested in something, then you naturally ask relevant questions to try to understand it. I call this a "conversation", so the key for me wasn't to contrive a package of open questions; it was just to have an interest in my prospect in order to understand their requirements and win the business. It is utterly amazing how many salespeople turn up to a meeting or take a phone call with a prospect and don't ask a single question. They just brain dump a pre-prepared blurb that sounds vaguely professional, thank the prospect for their time and hand over their business card on the chance they have any more questions. They often don't even bother talking to the person again and would rather follow up by email, which takes substantially longer, allowing them to spend their day hiding behind admin and remaining seemingly busy and shamelessly unproductive. The problem is more prevalent in recent years since we have become an email-driven society.

The flip side of effectively speaking to prospects is listening to them. Productive meetings are a two-way process and it is important to not only discuss the listening skills of a salesperson, but also the receptiveness of the people to whom we pitch.

Some prospects can make all the right signals, nodding and smiling through a presentation while holding your gaze; yet their minds are entirely absent. They may even ask the odd question to keep you talking so they can carry on not listening. This behaviour is not malicious and can be down to any number of reasons: their attendance may be compulsory yet they don't view it as a business critical meeting; they may be stressed about other issues that are more important; or they may have already selected another provider and are just turning up to tick the box. Whatever the reason, they are viewing my presentation as little more than a mental break and, if I pick up on it, then I bring it to their attention in the least confrontational manner possible so as not to spike their ego. One way to do this is to simply stop talking mid-flow during a pitch. I did this by accident once and couldn't believe it when the chap didn't even notice, sitting there in silence for a good five to six seconds until he realised. It was utterly surreal and, over time, I have refined this technique into something slightly different.

The problem with stopping talking is that the person quickly notices because they are responding to the patter. But, if I keep everything the same and completely change the subject mid sentence, then I can go on for much longer until they realise. When they finally suspect something isn't right and have no idea what is being said, then I apologise for losing my train of thought and ask them the last thing they remember. It can be a total eye-opener and, having experimented with this over the years, I often wonder to what degree anybody is ever listening. Most people seem to skip over information that doesn't fit with their agenda, despite not knowing whether it is relevant or not.

The important thing is to identify a lack of attention and do two things. First, ask them if they are genuinely interested in the product or the feature being described. It's sincere and important because their lack of interest suggests I am not fulfilling a need, and if that is the case, then they are not going to buy from me – or they just might not be involved in the decision so see little point in paying attention. This is useful information.

Second, if they are interested, then that's great but I want to understand what they need from me. Do they want me to summarise the key points, tell them the price in two minutes and let them go about their day? Better for us both that I know and give them what they need in the format they choose. After all they are just filtering my words to get to it. By connecting with their unspoken agenda I am able to build rapport and show that they can be honest and trust me to support them. Nowadays, I experiment with changing subject mid-sentence with friends, prospects, clients or anyone I think isn't listening to me because I would rather say nothing than talk to myself.

It is not compulsory for a prospect to listen and process what is being said, but it is absolutely compulsory for a salesperson to listen, and their results are a direct consequence of how well they are able to do so. There was once a girl on my team who was really lovely but simply incapable of listening. She was so wrapped up in herself that her world was about nothing more than sharing her amazingness with everybody. She enjoyed some sales success because she was charming with it, but suffice to say never exceeded the results of an average salesperson and missed the point that selling is about your client and not you. She was not unique, and I have worked with peers, even some with 20-years-plus sales experience, who wouldn't have the first clue how to ask a question and then stop talking long enough for the client to respond in full. They anticipate the answer and cut the client off, missing a lot of important information that they could use to close the deal. Surely it's the most simple and basic skill of all.

Ask the questions that you need to know to close your deal, then stop talking. I don't think it matters if they are all open questions – for example, "I would love to work with you on this project. Can you tell me a bit about what you are looking for and how you are going to make a decision?" Or closed questions, such as, "Will you choose a supplier this week?" or "Can I put you in touch with some internal references with whom we have worked recently?" Or even, "If we match all of these criteria can I work with you on this project?" The questions just need to be relevant. Is it really so hard? Maybe not for me, because I love doing good deals and am genuinely interested in what they are saying.

I want to take this a little further and share two gems that were gifted to me quite early in my career. Both of these principles share the credit for opening my eyes to the study of speaking and listening to my clients. It was explained to me that, to be a great salesman, I needed to "master the uncomfortable silence", so I started to build it into my meetings.

In the beginning it just felt awkward because I didn't understand when best to apply this technique. However, I never felt the urge to fill the silence because peoples' reactions were too fascinating. The first time I recognised its value was in one particular meeting, where shortly after finishing my short deck presentation, I decided to wait for the response − no matter how long it took. From the prospect's perspective, he was waiting for me to continue, but I had finished, so the silence endured as we looked at one another. It became so uncomfortable that I could not help but burst out laughing, which made him laugh, which made me laugh more. It was hilarious because the good laugh we had shared seemed to inject a sense of relaxation into the meeting and gave us a more solid foundation upon which to proceed.

I came to recognise that the uncomfortable silence has a place in many situations, but for me it is a wonderful technique to change, alter, readjust the pace or sentiment of a meeting. Previously, I described using it mid-flow in meetings with people who demonstrated a lack of interest. But the silence doesn't have to be a contrived stop to the conversation. It can be a period of extended thought or a natural break in a pitch, and can last as long as is necessary, but the point is that I wait for the prospect to continue. This can often lead the meeting into an entirely different direction that presents a new set of requirements based on their agenda. It is also useful in jovial presentations to change the feeling to a more serious tone in which to summarise my value proposition or close the deal. It's hard to explain to those with little meeting experience, but the uncomfortable silence seems to wipe the slate clean on all the points leading up to it.

Clearly it has an obvious place in price negotiation too, but my preference is to reserve this technique for less contrived applications. The skill to its mastery lies in understanding when it can be utilised to the maximum potential and, more often than not, it yields advantageous information about my meeting and prospect.

The second gem that was imparted to me was that I must be "the king of reasonable statements", because nobody can argue with what is reasonable. This principle is extremely helpful to me when developing a sales pitch, and it applies to all aspects of communicating with prospects. It is very difficult to counter a reasonable argument because it transpires that reasonable is non-confrontational, and this has been crucial in helping temper my naturally aggressive and competitive streak. I feel passionately that every single deal should be mine and sometimes have to be careful how this comes across. In tough and complex negotiations, or in front of a client whose ego is so out of line that it is aggravating me, then I use this principle as a great sanity check to everything that I say – openly discussing keys points as reasonable and unreasonable as opposed to acceptable and unacceptable.

Let me finish with a short story about the power of not filling an uncomfortable silence. My ex-boss and I had been working on closing a deal for several months. A substantial trial period had recently elapsed and the information gathered during this time was used as a yardstick upon which to base the final price for an annual contract. We agreed to have our closing meeting over lunch as it had been an intense process and had become quite close. It came to the point where the pleasantries were over and it was time to talk business. So our prospect asked us what conclusion we had come to regarding price, to which I replied that, based on his trial usage, it felt appropriate to settle on a number in the region of £10,000.

After an extended and deliberate pause, he asked if we had the capacity to spread the cost and bill him monthly. Although this was not usual practice, we were happy to agree to it, but in return asked for a commitment spanning two years rather than one. To help him justify the extended commitment we offered a 10% discount over the second year subscription. Again, he said nothing for quite some time and I could see my boss wanted to laugh but neither of us flinched. It felt like minutes as our future client rubbed his mouth and tipped his head back to the sky deep in thought. I wasn't quite sure why it took so much thought because it was only £10,000 per year and £9,000 for the second year. Regardless we were both happy to wait for a possible objection. Eventually he replied with, "OK, so £10,000 per month seems reasonable over two years as long as I can have it invoiced monthly." It took a nanosecond to register what had happened and we just smiled in agreement, shook hands and told him how happy we were to be working together.

We immediately ordered a bottle of champagne to celebrate a good deal and a pleasant process. We had expected to secure £10,000 per annum and walked out with £228,000 over 2 years. It didn't really affect the prospect at all. It was boom time and his firm was making hundreds of millions per year, but a 22.8 multiple on expected revenue from our side is nice business if you can get it for saying nothing at all.

#5 IN SUMMARY...

The ability to generate rapport, trust and sales by speaking to clients as an equal and in a language they understand, as well as LISTENING and responding to their objections while executing a defined sales process are basic and fundamental behaviours of a top salesperson. Most salespeople think they do it, but they don't, and it's often the key to maximising revenue opportunities as well as winning a deal if two products are similar.

6. THE COMPULSORY BASICS OF CLIENT MEETINGS

One of the first things I like to do when joining a new firm is to approach the existing top salesperson for guidance. They have already devised the most effective sales processes to overcome the challenges they face, and understanding this can save a lot of time. However, they may be reluctant to share this information, and this is fair enough because I have often felt the same way when approached by new starters. Early in my career I was a little more receptive and used to try to nurture my colleagues, but was always disappointed when their commitment fell short of what was promised and eventually concluded that there were more productive ways to spend my time. A common difference between top salespeople and the rest of their team is that they don't need constant nurturing. We learn the basic principles from the best and make them our own. All I really want to know from the current top salesperson is, high level, what to look out for and what they are doing differently. If I am lucky then they will share it, but ultimately I will get there myself with or without their input.

Regardless of how I must adapt to succeed, there is always the need to execute the same pre-defined sales discovery process when meeting potential clients. Before sharing how I do this, what follows is a list of personal principles, beyond a firm handshake and eye contact, which collectively have always given me an edge over the competition.

The first has been met with a little controversy over the years. When first starting in sales I spoke with a strong Southern English accent. My first boss recommended elocution lessons to improve the clarity of my speech and help gain acceptance in a class-orientated industry. It was great advice that has served me well since. Not only did it improve the clarity of my communication, but it has also helped me to control my breathing and pace of speech. I have maintained a more neutral accent ever since, but still sound like a farmer after a few beers.

Second, barring natural disaster or a delayed flight, I am not late to meetings – and being on time means 10 minutes early. It is the height of bad manners to turn up late to a meeting, but I know many salespeople who don't seem to care. This slack mind-set is one of the things, in my opinion, that brands them as average.

Third, I make a conscious effort to look good and not stand out or wear anything that might give someone a strong opinion about my appearance: no bling, gold necklaces, cartoon cufflinks or outrageous shirts or ties. The only opinion my clients should have is that I look smart and professional, and so I only wear neutral, tailored, classic clothes. This is of particular importance when selling in continental Europe, where people tend to be fashion conscious and make an effort to look smart. Shoes are key. There is little point having a beautiful suit and cheap shoes, and I must admit to being the first to judge a bad pair. A ritual that I have always followed is to give my suits to charity after each job and buy again for a new role. It holds something symbolic for me, like wiping the slate clean. The point is that looking and feeling good inevitably leads to delivering a better pitch. My office always has a spare suit, a couple of shirts, several ties and a pair of shoes on the off chance that I stay out all night, spill food on myself (it happens) or it pours with rain.

This was touched on in the previous chapter, but the fourth point is that I don't book a meeting without asking what to expect in terms of numbers attending, their job roles and the type of presentation they want to receive – a discussion, PowerPoint or live presentation? It is important to glean as much information prior to the meeting as possible and to try to understand the topics they want me to focus on, whether the pitch is competitive and what will be the deciding factors. Comprehensive pre-meeting sales discovery can sometimes swing the sale into my lap before I even turn up, because my presentation can be tailored to be as pertinent as possible. If they don't want to answer my questions at this stage then that is fine, it's just that this is often an overlooked opportunity and I make the most of it as a point of habit.

Also important is my mindset before a pitch. We have never met; they have a professional need for my service and, at this point, we are not friends. I am happy to small talk about my journey or the nice weather we are having, but don't take this as a sign to be over-familiar.

My memory for names is awful, so at the beginning of each meeting I lay everybody's business cards out to mirror the order in which they are sitting. If they don't have a card, then I take their email address and shortly after leaving send them a note thanking them for their time and asking a question. This instigates a response to which they have unwittingly attached their full details on their auto signature, including their direct telephone number. This immediately syncs to my contact database which links to everything, from mailing lists to the relationship management system. My secretary periodically scans my piles of business cards and sees what they relate to by referring to my diary.

When it comes to closing a deal, if a prospect doesn't respond within the pre-agreed time frame, then I rethink my position and move to a backup plan. My theory is that nobody delays good news, and so I take counter steps to disrupt a potential loss. On the flip side, the moment somebody agrees a deal, my immediate response is to thank them for their business and take steps to begin the process. This includes getting the contract, or letter of intent, signed as quickly as possible to block my competitors from making a counter-offer. I have won many deals after initially losing the mandate to a competitor by taking advantage of their complacency.

Finally, if a colleague or peer asks to attend one of my meetings, I make it clear that they will say nothing unless invited to contribute. There is nothing more ridiculous or counterproductive than people from the same company talking over one another, and all too often my client meetings have been completely disrupted by colleagues trying to add something that is totally unnecessary.

The above points are not compulsory but have always served me well. The following five stages of sales discovery, however, are compulsory – they apply to every deal and help me to ascertain the necessary information to secure the business.

Initial background: How they found me? This can tell a lot about who they know or what they may have heard already. Preferred meeting format and who is attending? Who decides the mandate, and are there any unforeseen complexities to the decision-making process such as budget, time frames or procurement authorisation? What is the time frame to mandate a supplier?

Establishing their needs: What is the exact opportunity on the table? Is it just this one, the first of many, or do they have the need for any of our other services? What are their specific requirements from this product and meeting? Do they have any preconceived concerns and objections or is there anything that they want me to focus on?

Establishing credibility: What do you know about us as a company? Shall I spend a few minutes telling you about us so we are all on the same page? This includes my personal experience and why we are best positioned to work with you. In return can you tell me about your company? This offers the opportunity to explore other areas of the business and the need for my services.

Full presentation of product: Following the process described in pitch preparation and focusing on the areas of interest already discussed.

Closing: Ask how they feel about the product and address any outstanding issues. Discuss the transparency of our pricing model, the value it represents and describe how easy it is to buy the product or sign up to the service. Is there additional information that will help them make a decision? For example, is an internal, external or peer reference useful? Should I coordinate with the legal team to give them some comfort with our terms of business?

My aim at this point is always to get any potential issues on the table that may slow the sales process or complicate the mandate, and then formulate action points together with the time frame. If the sales cycle is short or it is appropriate, I always summarise my points and pre-close the business by confirming that we have a deal when their outstanding issues have been addressed. Or, if everyone is already happy, then I ask for the business. For more complex sales processes that require several meetings, the structure is the same throughout the entire sales cycle. Each meeting addresses specific objections, pre-closes each point and confirms that, once their requirements are met, then the mandate is ours.

With the business discussion concluded, it's imperative always to ask for references and referrals. So many connections, deals and important information come from doing this, especially if you share a good rapport with your client, and it is often possible to push for multiple names as well as a direct introduction.

It doesn't always happen in this order, but it's not a correct process in my mind unless all these points have at least been addressed. One of the most important things that my compulsory basics demonstrate is that professional selling involves a process of intricately understanding your client and all aspects required to win their business. The only way to achieve this, as well as convey your own message, is to adhere to a process that aims for a balanced ratio of mutual communication throughout the meeting and sales cycle. It is not a brain dump and hope you win. Some of the worst perpetrators of not adhering to any formal process or even asking the correct questions are so-called senior salespeople who have become complacent and don't bother to execute a disciplined sales process to close a deal down as fast as possible.

#6 IN SUMMARY...

Understanding meeting dynamics and how to adapt accordingly, and always obtaining the maximum amount of information to close a deal at the earliest opportunity, are basic and fundamental behaviours of a top salesperson. Most salespeople don't do this well enough.

7. INVISIBLE REVENUE

"I don't get it… why do you always have the highest average price per unit in your sales number every month?" A colleague asked me this during a weekly sales meeting and I remember just looking at him thinking, no, you will never get it. Nice guy, but every month he struggled to meet his quota in a boom market.

There was no point explaining it to him because he lacked the desire to better himself. I learnt a long time ago that it is not possible to help people who do not want to help themselves. However, let me demystify the process of getting the maximum price. I ask the right questions, listen carefully to the answers, present my product in the best possible light and have the commercial awareness to translate what is being said into revenue. I also have the commercial awareness to ask questions regarding opportunities outside of the current deal. My ex-colleague just turns up for work and goes through the motions before heading home, whereas I treat my job and revenue as if it's my own company and my clients are happy to pay a premium to work with someone that they can trust to provide an exemplary service. Convincing them of this is just part of raising the value of my offering and being brilliant at The Basics.

Not leaving money on the table can be achieved in any number of ways. For example, you can extend a contractual period to lock the client down for longer, offer volume based discounts to encourage use of a service, or incentivise your client to use your product or service in different areas of their business. The options are endless and vary by product and industry.

However, these techniques for generating the maximum revenue from any given account are only applicable to a pre-established sales process. It is important to make a clear distinction between this, which I consider to be simply *maximising revenue*, and what I am referring to as *invisible revenue*. I have heard the concepts of maximising revenue and invisible revenue each explained in various ways over the years. The best way for me to explain how I personally separate the two concepts is to share an experience that happened to me while on holiday. By making a clear distinction between the two it has always allowed me to devise an effective selling strategy for each.

It was a typical summer weekend in a bustling seaside village, and parking was a nightmare. I decided that, rather than subject the whole family to sitting in the car in search of a parking space, I would drop them off and arrange to meet somewhere in the main high street. Thirty minutes or so later I called to check their whereabouts and we agreed to rendezvous in a small art gallery near the beach.

As I entered, everyone was deep in conversation with the owner about some artwork that she had recently acquired. On first impression, I found her quite loud and a little pushy, but I was more interested in heading to the beach so didn't pay much attention. Choosing not to get involved, I turned my back and decided to browse until they had finished. It was difficult not to overhear the owner explaining that this latest series of seven paintings was the last to ever be produced by a very famous local artist who was experimenting with a new brush technique. He was 93, and what was so remarkable was that he had produced paintings of the highest technical standard on his first attempt at a new technique, right at the end of his career. She seemed very passionate and the story, which was actually fascinating, made me wonder whether I hadn't been a little hasty to judge her.

Now, firmly focused on each painting, she pointed out the expertise and began to open my eyes to a new world. After some discussion with us all, she turned to me and asked if I were to pick one, then which would it be and why? It was difficult to tell whether she genuinely wondered, or whether this was just a beautifully executed sales process. It was irrelevant and likely both, but within a very short period of time I had grown to like her and her products. As I chose my favourite piece and explained the reasons, she interjected and explained that there was a seventh painting upstairs that she had been reserving for herself, but from what I had said it would likely be an even better option for me. She created a sense of exclusivity by making it clear that she wasn't keen to part with it, but would consider it if I felt strongly enough. Clever girl, but on inspection it didn't inspire me in the same way as the first painting. In fact, I had not just connected with the ingenuity of my original piece, but also two others, and it was becoming difficult to decide between all three.

I wanted to know more about her so I asked why she had opened the gallery, to which she explained that she had relocated from America to live in this tiny village on the south coast of England, primarily because she loved the local art and wanted to sell paintings to people who also feel a strong connection to it. She seemed genuine and offered a substantial discount for all three paintings, so I gave two to my parents and kept my favourite. There isn't a day goes by that I don't look at it, love it, and am happy to have had the opportunity to acquire it.

Did I need that painting or have any intention of buying it before I walked in? Was I the victim of a well-executed sales process or did she really mean what she was saying? I like to believe it was both and, whatever her motivation, I appreciated the passion with which she had presented herself. It was an emotional purchase but it is the sentiment behind the sales process that is most important. Did she establish and fulfil a need? No she didn't, she inspired a desire that I never knew I had, and this is the key to generating invisible revenue. Salespeople are spoon-fed in every course they attend, that in order to sell something they must establish a need. Do you? The best salespeople understand that establishing a need is the first step but only part of a more complex process. Sometimes you have to show people what they want. In business, this type of emotional purchase does not tend to happen because there must always be a commercially justifiable reason to buy something – but the process of achieving it is the same.

The way to inspire a desire in a professional business context is first to understand the profile of your prospect, as well as the world in which they operate. With a genuine grasp of the obstacles they face, it's important next to constantly probe and challenge how they do things and, in addition to addressing their conscious needs, be able to communicate on a level that explores all potential opportunities for revenue generation. Once an area of professional pain or inefficiency has been identified, it is then a matter of solving the problem they never knew they had and attaching a monetary value to it. It goes from a nice-to-have concept to a need-to-have, justifiable business-critical solution that can be sold.

One of the most effective ways to do this, especially when selling highly specialist products, is to leverage internal product or industry specialists *appropriately* and have them talk to your prospect. There is a difference between this and what was described earlier as having specialists compensate for a salesperson's inadequate understanding of their product. If the specialists' presence in these discussions is used correctly, the sales job is simply to translate what is being said into tangible revenue-generating income for both businesses.

To demonstrate these two processes working in tandem, let me describe how, over a 12-month window, I managed to overturn a decision that took my company from being blacklisted from any mandate, to becoming the preferred supplier to one of the largest investment banks in the world.

Any deal in which this particular account contributed to the mandate process was considered a dead loss to my company, as we had been excluded from pitching for their business. The problem we faced, as a team and a business, was that operating in a market with such a huge player against us would seriously impact our revenues, so I started making enquiries and began the process of reversing the damage.

There were three levels of decision-maker. The first was the ground level. These were the users of our service who sought to mandate the suppliers deal-by-deal. Seeking multiple quotes for each deal wasn't the most efficient way of doing things because they had to run the same pitch process every time the need arose, and this took a lot of repeated effort over the course of a year. The second, more senior decision-makers were two business-practice Vice Presidents (VPs). Their responsibility was to analyse a number of business processes and ensure they operated efficiently. One of these VPs was focused on business efficiency and the other was responsible for integrating new IT platforms and ensuring that they conformed to their strict legal responsibilities. Finally, sitting on the highest rung of the ladder, was the Head of Investment Banking in Europe. He had final say on any company-wide policy, but all business justification had to be formulated before reaching him for approval. There were two ways to approach this account because the decision to exclude us had come from the middle tier of responsibility.

The first approach was to go to the top – a person whom I was unlikely to reach given his seniority and who would surely frown upon a request to override his own team. The second was to start below the VPs, gain some trust and rapport, then approach them with successful case studies and ask to wipe the slate clean. The latter seemed a less treacherous route, so I called some friends in a different bank, who worked closely with this blacklisted company, to ask them for a warm introduction to some of the low level players.

It didn't take long to convince these new contacts to work

with us on a couple of deals, and with two successful case studies it felt appropriate to ask for an internal referral to the VPs, explaining the good work we had done to date. I was a little apprehensive calling the VP of Business Strategy, but to my surprise she was lovely and happy to discuss the historic relationship between our companies. It turns out that the team below had sent a glowing reference in my support and it had opened the door to a frank and productive meeting. She explained what had happened in the past and generously gave me the opportunity to win her trust going forward.

We met several times over the coming weeks and she invited me to pitch to the remainder of the decision-making team to explain why, despite our historic differences, we were the best company to be working with. Her counterpart, the VP of IT, was also a really decent and straight-talking person. We collectively agreed that in return for a healthy concession on the price, my company would be given the opportunity to demonstrate our superior capabilities on a couple of large upcoming deals. It was the perfect opportunity to prove myself and I spent a great deal of time learning about this company and how it positioned itself in the market against competing firms. As we grew to trust one another, they began to adopt me as part of the team and often asked my advice when dealing with other salespeople and similar products.

Back in the office, a political war was raging over assuming control of this account, but I had absolutely no interest in this squabble for accreditation because the reversal of our hopeless position was benefitting everybody. It is very difficult to argue with someone who has turned a dead loss into a substantial win. Over the coming months this account had grown to be our biggest revenue generator in Europe and, having gained a more senior level of trust, it was time to ask their support to meet with the head of investment banking. The aim was to become the preferred supplier to the firm, but there had to be a strong business justification to arrange this meeting.

In support of this, I devised a price platform for the entire bank in Europe. If they agreed to give me preferential supplier status, their total volume of work meant I could offer the best price in the industry for all their deals. It would mean that they would hold a competitive advantage over similar banks in the industry because they could then offer my market-leading service to their clients on a cheaper basis than anybody else. All agreed with my proposal and gave their blessing but, foreseeing a potential objection, I was advised to gain pricing approval first from the Procurement team.

Dealing with Procurement is normally a predictable process in that their primary goal is to save money. They look bad if they go into a negotiation and fail to get a discount, so I always compensate for this by slightly inflating my price and arguing its value before agreeing to the original price. The harder I negotiate, the greater the victory in their eyes when I concede, and with the meeting reaching its conclusion exactly as expected, the door was open to present to the most senior decision-maker in Europe.

It was only ever going to be a short meeting, and to support this I was sitting with a deck of evidence that made his decision an easy one. With the blessing and legacy at every level to support promoting us to preferred supplier status, I could further demonstrate tangible cost savings and business efficiencies by doing so. After 12 months of providing an exemplary service, all he would really be looking for was that I was a straight guy who understood his business and wouldn't get it wrong. The decision really couldn't, and didn't, fall any other way.

From his perspective, did he need to do this deal? No, he could have kept operating just fine and never been aware of any detrimental impact on his business by not streamlining this process. I brought it to his attention and inspired him to improve it by leveraging everything at my disposal and demonstrating a sound business justification by understanding all the challenges he faced at every level of his business.

From my perspective, as a salesman, I could have just kept picking off low-level deals, met the obvious need and hit my target. That would still have been a considerable win from our historic position, but it never even crossed my mind: I always work towards the Holy Grail, which is a flow of uncontested deals. This type of deal secures all their business and also frees my time to focus on doing the same deal elsewhere. Now, consider the two potential approaches to this dead-loss account that I could have taken in the beginning to try to circumvent the VPs. The choice was either to go over their heads by contacting the head of European banking, or start beneath them to build a strong foundation upon which to proceed.

Many salespeople would have chosen the former approach because they don't have the necessary sales skills to work through the latter and are lazy. They would have taken a nothing-to-lose mentality that would almost certainly have been met with a lack of result. Finally, consider the benefit of the latter approach in the type of meeting that I had with the ultimate decision-maker. The first was asking to override the experiences of his trusted team and giving me a shot to work with them, the second was presenting him with an irrefutable opportunity to improve his business that had the support of all involved.

This is professional selling by a top salesperson. It is not only identifying the immediate opportunities and generating the maximum revenue, but it's also identifying and closing invisible revenue by inspiring a desire, assigning a quantifiable value to it, demonstrating that it's actually a legitimate business need, and closing it. Could I have done any of this without engrossing myself into their business and the challenges they faced? It simply would not have been possible, and just as satisfying is the fact that, several years later, I am still friends with both VPs.

Before moving on, I want to share a couple of simple techniques that have helped me to clarify opportunities and maximise revenue in certain situations.

The first is that, in a negotiation scenario, I have never found a more effective tool than a basic sliding scale to isolate objections, quantify all the parameters that affect the price and to restate my value proposition. Drawing a line across a blank page, I place what is acceptable to each of us on opposite ends and explain from the offset that splitting the difference isn't acceptable. Starting from the median price demonstrates that any concession is only slight, and I refer to the new scale, which is 50% up from my original position. This needs to be justified or it looks childish and, having done a thorough sales job leading up to this point, it's the correct opportunity to restate why we are worth more than this mid-point price. The buyer can object strongly, which is exactly the intended response, because this forces them to justify their position and typically exposes their genuine reasons for not agreeing a deal. Once on the table, it's a matter of assigning a tangible value to each objection and positioning them on the scale relative to the final price. With a clear picture, we now have a visual framework upon which to resolve objections and demonstrate the cost implication of each.

If the salesperson has done a good job up to this point, then the client will understand that for the deal to happen, a compromise will need to be reached. One way to do this is to exchange non-price related benefits to my company, in return for a small discount to theirs. This is the best opportunity not just to recoup what is lost, but also to up-sell substantially from the original price point. I now suggest a list of everything that my company would need in order to make a small concession acceptable and, believe me, it is a substantial list, which might include a guarantee of future work, an increase in the contract term, a number of referrals, an official reference on headed paper, a comment in an industry journal citing us as key to operational success, free internal marketing to relevant people and so on. Then, I say nothing and wait for them to talk.

More often than not the buyers will already have an idea of what an acceptable compromise might be, and this is their opportunity to show their final cards. Even if acceptable, I try to squeeze out at least one more incremental benefit for my company. The value of many non-price related concessions can be far greater than small concessions could ever match – a favourite of mine being to swap a discount on this occasion for the promise of future work. It's a win-win scenario, which is the nucleus of any good deal, and the sliding scale helps me be clear about the process.

Another useful technique to maximise revenue, especially in a new market where the price levels are as yet undefined, is to itemise and charge for all aspects of a service rather than roll them into an all-encompassing price. What is the difference between a £650,000 bill and an £850,000 bill when the company has just made £1.5billion and could not have done it without your services? One answer is £200,000, but another answer is "Who cares?" They just made £1.5billion. The ethos in the financial industry has always been to just get the job done and we all make a lot of money. So, companies have made a pastime out of charging what someone is willing to pay, rather than the actual cost, plus a fixed margin. They do this by itemising and assigning a price to every aspect of their service, knowing that the client will likely run up a huge bill that will be the basis for negotiating down to what they are willing to pay.

For example, imagine giving your client, who is on a tight deadline, a special keyboard that allows them to do their job faster. You tell them to type away, but every time they hit a key it costs £0.20. If a client just needs to get a job done in a tight time frame to generate £1.5billion, then they could not care less about the pennies every time a key is struck. Furthermore, if this client and 20 others all go into a room, which they have also paid to use, and type around the clock for four days, then the result is the most obscene price imaginable. It is justifiable in terms of where it came from, but really is just a starting point upon which to negotiate. The bill, despite being grossly over-inflated for the service provided, is viewed as minor in comparison to the overall value achieved by doing the deal, and the top salespeople always manage to charge and settle on the highest fee because they are most effective in raising the value proposition to the client.

Maximising the return from a client isn't just about closing the deal for the best price, but it is a mindset that follows through to all aspects of the sales process. In this respect, I don't consider that free product trial periods are ever actually free.

Anything free tends to be wide open to abuse, and the purpose of a free trial is to provide the salesperson a window of opportunity within which to sell their product. It is not a give-and-forget type mentality; rather it is the best opportunity that a salesperson will ever get to connect with their prospect, so I never just hand my service over for free. The prospect has to explain to me why they need it and the process that their company must follow in order to buy it once the trial period expires. I stay in constant communication throughout the process to ensure it concludes favourably. Approaching free trial periods with this mentality ensures the highest possible ratio of conversion from prospect to paying client.

Finally, the most effective sales strategy for maximising revenues and identifying invisible revenue, is to ensure other team members understand these techniques so they too can recognise potential business opportunities. By creating a heightened commercial awareness across all departments, the likelihood of finding untapped revenue is greatly increased and the business is being driven forward on every level.

#7 IN SUMMARY...

Understanding the dynamics of the sales process and the mechanisms that identify and generate revenue, engrossing yourself in the client's world and taking a global view of every opportunity, maximising the value of your product and therefore its sale price, volume and contract length to lock-out competition, and monitoring deal execution to identify other chargeable opportunities, are all basic and fundamental behaviours of a top salesperson. Most salespeople don't ask the right questions to unveil these opportunities and leave money on the table.

8. NETWORKING

With a career focused predominantly on the banking sector, the steep decline in market activity during an economic downturn tends to have an inordinately detrimental effect on my ability to perform. This is not just due to reduced deal volumes, but mainly to the consequence of the enormous budgetary cuts and mass redundancies that follow in tough times. The impact is that the clients with whom I have spent years building trusted relationships are now no longer in employment and, on two such occasions after periods of sustained contractual absence, I returned to find that my entire contact deck had been all but decimated. It needed to be quickly rebuilt, and experience has taught me the most efficient mechanisms to regenerate my network and convey a message to a lot of people.

Shortly after returning from a 12-month absence, my efforts to reconnect with my previous best clients had amounted to nothing. It was apparent that my contact base had been devastated by redundancies and, in the face of uncertainty, the others had voluntarily moved to other finance-related roles. I was at a loss, so decided to follow my normal ritual when faced with a professional road block — I cleared my desk of everything but the phone, took a couple of sheets of clean A4 paper from the printer, a fine-tip roller ball pen and started calling anyone who might be in a position to help. Success in this particular type of sales role comes to those who have two levels of contacts at their disposal. The first is to know a lot of junior-based prospects who would be responsible for collecting quotes from suppliers and presenting their findings up the chain, and the second is to have the necessary senior-based relationships to influence the mandate for any deal favourably.

At the forefront of my mind was the fact that I am just one person and that, in order to multiply quickly, the first people to identify are "Connectors". A Connector is someone who is always in the mix and perfectly placed to introduce me to a number of key contacts. They are sometimes referred to as Champions, although a Champion to me is a stronger term that is used to describe someone who can be relied on to recommend my services. The most obvious Connectors in this instance were the senior directors who could introduce me to those remaining on their teams, but cold-calling players of this stature was a risky strategy – far better to contrive an introduction from a Connector to guarantee a warm reception.

A good ex-client and friend had recently updated his profile on LinkedIn, so I dropped him a line at his new firm, explained my predicament and asked for help. His ex-boss was still one of the most senior bankers in his division and my friend was happy to facilitate a meeting. It was just a matter of following The Basics from here on in and establishing rapport and credibility to get his approval to meet with the remaining team. The series of introductions he made allowed me to identify the next Connector within his team, who passed me on, and this process continued as they all tended to know each other.

Time to find Connector number two. Another friend, who was now CEO of a large corporate company with a client-base that mirrored my own, agreed to introduce me formally to a number of his most senior contacts. Same process as before, and within one week I was back to four to five meetings a day with a list approaching a hundred or so key people who were in a position to include me in all the upcoming pricing requests. Moving with senior level recommendation made every contact a warm one, and within a month a flow of quote requests began to hit my inbox once again.

My philosophy on networking has always been that I am just one person and need to recruit others to pass on my message. This goes further to explain why unique visual imaging and sound bites are so important when talking about my product, because this message is more likely to be retained and passed on exactly as it is told. My ultimate aim is to create as many clones of myself as possible, and those I covet most to pass on my message are the people of influence within the industry.

To continue, after amassing a community of junior contacts, it was time to move on to the more important process of building more meaningful relationships with the directors who mandate deals. It isn't realistic to know them all, so my attention was focused on a handful of key players who could offer me the maximum potential leverage when required. These people are the primary target for every salesperson and often the most difficult characters to get close to. It is easy to get distracted and spend time with less influential and more amenable people, so to ensure this doesn't happen I consciously allocate the majority of my entertainment budget to specific people, and then look for the opportunities to spend it on them. This keeps the right people in the forefront of my mind and ensures that my efforts are rewarded should I need to hard close a deal or pull one deal back from the brink of a loss.

The best Connectors can sometimes be found in unusual places, and the skill is to identify them as they cross your path. A good example was a guy who worked in a completely unrelated division of my account and whom I randomly met on a night out. He offered to put me on his social media contact list, which read like a who's who of the industry and I found myself invited out on the town with key clients twice a week. It was pure gold, and not just a work-related list, but a recurring party invitation where everybody had a good time. Another example is the Sales Directors of similar companies to my own. They are not just useful for cross-marketing opportunities and to share ideas, but also because between us we are collectively no more than one degree of separation from everybody else in the industry. By expanding my network in multiple avenues, there is very seldom the need to cold call prospects, and this networking strategy is entirely transferable to other types of sales role.

A consequence of selling a product low on the adoption curve is that there is always an extensive process of education before prospects begin to trust and accept the concept. It begins by communicating the benefits as well as demonstrating successful case studies to as many people as possible, as quickly as possible, and an effective way to achieve this is not only with large presentations at industry specific conferences, but also by setting up short group presentations to each of the key industry corporations. It is a good strategy to make contact with the relevant heads of department and either offer a short group presentation at their offices, or lay on a lunchtime educational presentation in one of our conference rooms and supply the catering.

A good example of covering hundreds of relevant people at once was a training event I attended in New York. Once a year every associate level banker globally, in a tier one investment bank, flies to New York for the whole of August to develop new skills and network with one another. On discovering this I arranged to fly in and present at this conference as my new technology was relevant to every single one of the 1100 people in attendance. I then threw the mother of all parties for everyone that evening. With the help of the 200 in attendance, my bar bill was the single biggest expense of my career, but it was paid for several times over from the revenues we gained from doing it.

A slightly different take on this is that I always look to host regular focus groups with a handful of key market individuals, as another way to network with buyers and influencers in an industry. These specialist gatherings amongst peers are often well attended, help me to stay at the forefront of future developments and identify invisible revenue. They also ensure I don't miss any opportunity to attend and present at larger industry events, and can also make sure that my details are included on their internal resource database, which is visible to all employees within their companies. This is a superb and often overlooked marketing opportunity where simply being listed is sometimes enough to automatically include your company in processes that you knew nothing about.

It is always useful to swing as many resources in my favour as possible so, in tandem with covering the obvious external parties, it is important to align everything else that could possibly work in the background to throw up opportunities. The next logical place to look is internally within my own company. My customer support teams are invaluable and, as previously mentioned, I actively train them to identify potential revenue-generating situations, as well as to understand the importance of passing on new leads. They are perfectly placed to do so because they spend the majority of their days helping people who didn't play a part in the decision-making process, but who might be in that position in the future. It would be an unforgivable missed opportunity not to make the most of this and channel this flow of information in my direction. Likewise, marketing and advertising teams are an obvious source of qualified contacts, and I like to work closely with them to ensure that a consistent, sales-based message – based entirely on unique selling points – flows throughout all the material that they circulate within the industry.

The resource that is potentially the most lucrative is my own sales team. They are already working with their own clients, who will likely know their counterpart in my accounts, and it can be a fantastic source of warm referrals. This stretches well beyond my own regional office, and I have helped many colleagues in other countries by leveraging my client base to close cross-border deals or make introductions. The best time to take advantage of this is when the company, regardless of location, has just won a large mandate such as the preferred supplier status mentioned in the previous chapter. Shortly after closing this deal, my contacts in Europe helped open the flow of business to our New York office. I flew over to oversee the process and the meetings that were arranged with the internal support and recommendation of the London office led to a similar discussion regarding all their North American-based business.

A less obvious internal resource can be in setting-up or leveraging strategic partnership channels with other firms in the industry. These partnerships are formed with the intention of producing a mutually beneficial business relationship that is stronger together than standing apart. So I have no issue either leveraging these relationships, no matter how loose, or identifying and agreeing these partnerships with like-minded firms. These relationships can be extremely beneficial and an easy way to generate more revenue for myself and the company.

In summary, these are some of the aspects I consider when joining a new industry or rebuilding a damaged network. The time taken to do this is dramatically reduced if I identify the correct connectors and align all the other resources toward my success. This process will not apply to every sales role, but the point I am making is that there is a little more to it than picking up the phone each day and calling the odd prospect. I want to finish by repeating two things already touched upon in previous chapters, but that are also relevant in the context of networking.

It is a good strategy to always watch how other successful people do things, and one such salesperson was a master at working a conference room. I have never seen anyone move so brutally through a group of people asking what they do and, if they were not relevant, wishing them well and moving on. It was the opposite of my style, which was to take an interest in people. His style made me cringe, but at the end of the event he always had far more and far better contacts than anybody else. I needed to adapt.

None of this is possible without shamelessly asking for referrals at every opportunity. Clients, prospects, people in general, are often blissfully unaware that they know someone who could be of use to me. It is my responsibility to identify who they know and leverage these useful relationships.

IN SUMMARY... #8

The ability to effectively utilise all the available resources to communicate with the market, and quickly instil credibility and the product message to a large number of people, while identifying and focusing the majority of your efforts on key decision-makers and influencers, are all basic and fundamental behaviours of a top salesperson. Most salespeople just contact the obvious players and have little idea of how to truly leverage everything at their disposal.

9. MAKING PEACE WITH MY EGO

My greatest challenge when dealing with unnecessarily difficult clients has always been to temper my response. As a result, I have had to develop various mechanisms to ensure that a clash of personalities will not negatively impact my business deals. One such mechanism, described in an earlier section, has been to benchmark my verbiage according to whether or not it is reasonable. However, some instinctive responses run a little deeper, and understanding how to manage them requires you to detach from a situation to view it from an entirely different perspective. The following is an example of how I learnt to understand and embrace my ego to make more money from buyers who aren't in control of theirs.

I was pitching to a buyer on a power trip like no other. Over the course of several months, he was unapologetic about turning up late, if at all, and was rude and aggressive at the slightest hint of disagreement. Meetings would typically start with him explaining how busy and important he was, and then telling me exactly what he wanted me to do. An example might be that to make a decision, he would like me to compile a series of special spreadsheets for him or redraft the proposal format. He constantly pricked my ego and sense of injustice because he would rarely look at the finished documents. His difficult stance and sense of self-importance were so unbearable it was becoming questionable whether the business was worth the grief it entailed. There is a clear distinction between a good negotiator and an egomaniac, and this chap was taking the latter to the extreme.

My boss had joined our meetings to help manage the process, but also struggled to accept the way this prospect conducted himself. We were determined it would never break our spirits and remained consummate professionals, gently handling every false objection and making him feel important. One day, however, we found ourselves wanting to walk. His refusal to acknowledge our efforts to date and demand for yet another set of unnecessary documentation before he would consider our proposal had pushed us over the edge. Back at the office, we discussed the situation and concluded that we would see this through to the end but, to help bear the injustice, we would need to find a better way to cope.

We decided that the best way to handle this situation was to calculate the cost of pandering to this buyer's excessive demands, and then find a way to charge him for it later. This new strategy not only gave us an added incentive to keep pushing for the deal, but it also meant we would be able to view his requests in a different way – as a legitimate new business opportunity. Besides helping us manage his behaviour on an ongoing basis, this new approach had inadvertently taught me one of the most invaluable sales lessons of my career - that I could control my emotional response to ego-based buyers by changing my perspective. The fact that he would be paying for each extraneous demand helped me to re-engage with a more positive attitude, allowing me to focus on the only thing that mattered – securing his business. We now needed to find a way to close the deal.

Questioning his methods was tantamount to commercial suicide and he always became aggressive. My naivety was not realising that you can never build rapport with egomaniacs by challenging them. He needed adoration and demanded his subjects pay obeisance. To win the business, we needed to acknowledge that he was "granting" us the business. The ego buyer is a god in their mind, but the one thing they all seem to respond to is *suggestion*. So to manage and close him, we would loosely suggest an idea, often by telling half a story with an obvious ending and letting him finish the train of thought. We would package the story as the latest trend or market insight, or even better suggest it was what their biggest competitor was doing and then just let it sink in. The objective is always to let them feel like it is their idea because, in their mind, all good ideas, and anything productive that happens, can only originate from them. It is easy to gauge the success of this tactic because at the end of the meeting, you just conveniently forget what they have said and ask them to repeat it. Then, the killer blow is to congratulate them for bringing such ingenuity to the process and be excited to help them make it happen. They feel great and in control of their minions, so the door is as good as open to send the invoice.

Ego-driven buyers and sellers are predictable, which greatly limits their ability to orchestrate good business. By understanding that my emotional response was nothing more than my ego clashing with theirs, it has helped me to develop the tools to connect with these characters and use their inadequacies to my advantage. It can often be the easiest sale you will ever make, and since the above example, I have enjoyed specialising in selling to ego-based decision-makers.

IN SUMMARY... #9

The ability to control your emotional responses so they don't clash with those of your prospects, and therefore make rational business decisions based on what is best for yourself and the company, is a basic and fundamental behaviour of a top salesperson. Most salespeople lack the self-awareness to recognise when this is happening and it often leads to lost business or doing a bad deal.

10. HUNGRY, GREEDY AND NEVER GIVE UP

It is hard for me to accept that anyone else would give a better service or take more pride in delivering a professional, well-executed job. A consequence of this mentality is that I assume every deal should be mine and, if the decision falls the wrong way, I refuse to accept a loss in the first instance. There are a number of tactics that can be employed to pull a deal back, and I don't relent until absolutely all avenues have been exhausted. Recovering deals from this position has been crucial to my success over the years, and what follows are a couple of experiences that highlight the importance of not giving up.

There have been countless occasions when clients have insisted upon a set of compulsory requirements from my product or service, only to realise these apparent deal-breakers were nothing more than the result of being misinformed by a competitor. It can be a very difficult task to challenge the infallible beliefs of a belligerent company director, but it is not always a lost cause. The most satisfying of all these was a meeting that took place at the headquarters of a large UK corporate just outside of London. There were four people in attendance – the two bankers who had invited me, as well as the Head of Legal Services and the Head of Information Technology (IT) from the corporate who required our service. It was a competitive pitch and we were second to the table. The first company to pitch had done a good job of undermining my product beforehand. They had learnt to adapt from previous losses, demeaning our technology and spinning their own in a clever way. The message left with the prospect was not entirely accurate, but they felt absolutely resolute in their understanding of the facts.

As usual, I opened the meeting by asking if there was anything they would like me to focus on. Pre-armed and confident that my system lacked the necessary attributes, they asked me to describe our protocols for handling document security. Shortly after beginning, both prospects from the corporate adopted defensive, closed body language that suggested they didn't like what they were hearing. They cut me short with a question on whether we could protect a certain function from users. When I explained that we couldn't, the Head of Legal shouted, "What? You can't even do that?" She then looked at the bankers who had invited me and asked, "Why have you bothered to bring these people here when they can't even do the most basic function?"

They squirmed in their seats as she looked back at me, insisting, "Let's just stop now. I don't even see the point of carrying on with this." Her reaction was so extreme and inappropriate it was more befitting a child throwing a tantrum than a professional in a business pitch.

Without wanting to respond inappropriately or sabotage

the opportunity, I just sat there and treated everybody to an extra-long uncomfortable silence to give the room the opportunity to reflect on how ridiculous her outburst had been. My lack of response or need to fill the silence ensured we all understood each other and that I wasn't going to tolerate a second outburst of this kind. It had taken me two hours by train to reach this office and I wanted my opportunity to pitch, so eventually I continued with a series of illuminating questions and reasonable statements.

"I am sorry, I am just a little confused. Before we wrap this up, do you mind if I ask if you know of a technology that *can* provide the features you require?" This would get us on the same page and tell me what she thought she knew. She blanket repeated the details of my closest competitor, so it became clear what had happened and how to recover it. Before a constructive conversation could begin, it was important to empathise with her position so that she would drop her defensive stance and be receptive to my response, so I proceeded in a direct and sincere tone: "I understand your concerns regarding interface security, and in fairness they are the same concerns shared by all clients in your position, but having just travelled for two hours to be here I would appreciate the opportunity to spend at least a couple of minutes talking conceptually about the limitations of *all* technologies in the market place. If you don't feel convinced after this, then let's wrap up."

Explaining that since we host the majority of transactions in the market and are the preferred supplier to the largest banks in the world, it was reasonable to assume that we met this objection every day and wouldn't be regarded in such high esteem if there was a technological hole in our system. She had fallen for a slightly misleading and well-worded pitch, which ended minutes before my arrival, but I didn't want to spike her already inflamed ego by confronting her with this. The objection she thought she had was not a limitation of our system, but an accepted risk associated with all products in existence, so the discussion now focused on the realm of technological limitations, rather than any perceived failing of my system. It turned out to be a long meeting, and my non-defensive stance began to tip the balance in our favour. Careful not to acknowledge my competition, I was able to isolate the issue and, with all other things being equal, pre-close the opportunity on the premise that I could prove the accuracy of my explanations.

Despite their scepticism, this was quickly resolved when the relevant experts on both sides were allowed to talk. It was a matter of simply following The Basics that resulted in recovering this deal. It turned out to be one of the largest European M&A transactions of the year, and we worked together, as their preferred supplier, on two further occasions. Although sometimes necessary, basing an entire pitch on directly disparaging the competition is a dirty way to sell. Far better, in my opinion, is to focus on the unique points of your own product and never acknowledge competing companies unless asked to compare. In the above example, the prospect was blissfully unaware that I knew exactly who had pitched before me and exactly how to counter their position. This deal was a good example of retaining my position from the back foot.

The next example demonstrates how I recovered from a loss and, once again, shows the importance of executing The Basics at every stage of the sales process, because you just don't know what can happen.

It is imperative not to leave any stone unturned in identifying and connecting with influential parties and decision-makers. This was a ground-breaking deal because it was the first time that a technology such as the one we offered was to be used within the Asian region – and it would be the example that all others would follow. The identity of the company for sale was a closely guarded secret, and the pitch process was being coordinated entirely through the advising bank. As always, I sought a senior-level referral from the bankers in London to their counterparts in Asia and never considered that the decision would not fall in my direction. In support of this, I removed any opportunity for price objections by offering a 50% discount for this first deal. The discount was justified, as we were also in the process of acquiring a company in Hong Kong, so securing a flow of business from Asia's largest player was a nice platform upon which to launch.

Meeting with the deal team in their Hong Kong headquarters, we agreed the terms, and afterwards I headed back to the office to prepare the contract, which would be signed the next day. We arranged another meeting for the following morning, in which they would give me back the signed contract and I would deliver a short marketing presentation to the entire division. Everything went like clockwork, and after our second meeting I had the chance to connect with the most senior bankers in the division and organise a dinner that evening.

With the contract in place, we started the process of executing the deal. On this particular evening the time difference was killing me. I remember lying in bed and waking at 4am when my blackberry buzzed with an email from my customer service team in London, saying that the deal was being taken off our system and placed onto a competitor's. My body surged with adrenaline like someone had taken something sacred. I instructed my team not to remove anything from our system until they heard from me again. With no sleep for the remainder of the night, at 8am I called the bankers and arranged to meet. At 8:30am we met in their lobby and they explained that somehow the competition had managed to identify the corporate and call them directly with the offer to host the deal for free. They were also up to their old tricks, demeaning our technology and promising things they couldn't deliver. These bankers were too junior and didn't have the authority to insist that we worked on the deal so, with the help of the senior bankers from dinner the night before, I managed to arrange a short meeting with the Managing Director of the entire division.

She was a busy, no-messing, straight-shooter, and I explained my position and the importance of this deal. We were their preferred supplier in Europe, and it made no commercial sense to risk working with a company who had a fraction of our credentials. She was no stranger to the pitching process and said that she would make a phone call to the corporate, but it might help if there was something I could do on price. I offered to cap the cost just above our break-even for this deal in exchange for their next deal, and she approved. None of this would have been possible without identifying and connecting with the senior bankers the day before. For the sort of money involved I was certain that the corporate would not go against their most senior advisers, and at 11am HK time we resumed work on the deal.

Besides senior-level support, the best defence to counter another salesperson taking my deals is to start the process of execution immediately after closing the deal. It is important to mobilise your team and coordinate with the client so that, should someone like me swoop in and try to sabotage the deal, it is simply too much hassle for the corporate to stop the process we have begun. The Holy Grail is to have them share some confidential information related to the deal because in this instance they are highly unlikely to breach their security and change supplier, regardless of who gets involved.

This way of working doesn't apply to every product and deal but, in my experience, it is preferable to start working on the promise that the contract will be signed in due course. The main driving force is that the contract can take time to negotiate, and this is a window in which the deal is still exposed to attack. The above example was recovered using a two-pronged approach. Not only had we already received their confidential data and the company was unaware of this, but I also had the most senior person on the advisory deal team relay this message to the corporate. It was a compelling case that outweighed any desire to save a few dollars, and the resulting deal still made my company money in the face of a free alternative.

You can't win them all, but I work on the assumption that "no" often doesn't mean "no". On the heartbreaking occasions when a mandate doesn't fall my way and there really is no chance of recovery, I wish them well and offer my support if, at any point, the process doesn't go as smoothly as anticipated. It is amazing how often a random phone call is made asking for guidance. Finally, I take note of when a contract or process has expired and make sure to reconnect and stay fresh in their minds for the next piece of business.

#10 IN SUMMARY...

Being hungry, greedy and never giving up are basic and fundamental behaviours of a top salesperson. The best salespeople execute a thorough sales process that covers every aspect of the decision-making dynamic so, if faced with a loss or competitive counter-offer, they can leverage their knowledge of the decision-making process to override the decision and secure the mandate.

CONCLUSION

The Basics are my personal formula for sales success. My aim in sharing these principles is to demonstrate that a professional sales process, as seen through the eyes of a top salesperson, is more than just turning up, showing a product to the obvious candidates and then going home. Rather, the process of selling is a well-contrived set of actions that puts me in the best possible position to succeed.

It is fair to say that the only time things have ever gone wrong for me can be explained by my not adhering to this set of personal rules. Many of these principles overlap to support one another, but there are three common threads that run throughout: I am better at leveraging what is available to me, I am better prepared to succeed, and I identify and close business that others don't see. The Basics help me to clarify the process of doing this and are the reason I consider that sales execution is the easiest part of my job. The next section discusses a far greater challenge – handling the many inter-company obstacles that come as part of being the top salesperson.

Section 3

Navigating the sales environment

*" **I**f you pick the right people and give them the opportunity to spread their wings and put compensation as a carrier behind it you almost don't have to manage them."*

Jack Welch, General Electric

INTRODUCTION

Every sales team operates differently. Some companies, notably large corporates, are highly organised and have defined processes that dictate how to pitch a product, as well as protocols for interacting with other teams within the organisation. In contrast, other companies choose to treat their salespeople as if they are self-employed and only dictate the amount of revenue and margin they expect per annum.

There are advantages and disadvantages to each approach. For example, a large corporation may appear to run like clockwork, yet over-complicate the simplest of tasks by laying down unnecessary red tape that is detrimental to productivity. For more autonomous sales environments, which are most common in teams that comprise of senior salespeople, it can be productive to have the freedom to make independent business decisions, but there can be catastrophic consequences if there is little managerial authority to enforce the basic rules of engagement between peers. A well-run sales environment has a healthy balance of both, where an organised and defined approach provides clear boundaries, yet still offers the more experienced salespeople the freedom to do good business as they see fit. In my experience this encourages the best results from the team as the top salespeople lead by example, driving the product into the market and monitoring the client feedback to further develop and dominate.

Regardless of team structure, all sales teams come with their own unique dose of internal egos and inter-company politics. In a healthy and highly productive company, the Sales Director keeps the impact of politics on the sales team to a minimum, shielding them from internal struggles and focusing their efforts on generating revenue. In less well-managed environments, where lots of money is at stake, lack of boundaries, company politics and strong, unruly personalities can sometimes cripple productivity. The biggest casualties in these scenarios are typically the top salespeople as they are constantly dragged into pointless battles with those looking to feed off their book of business. Having worked in all of the above situations, and fallen foul of poor management and company politics during my career, I learnt to employ a simple, unemotional approach to those who seek to distract me from realising my goals.

Whatever struggles there may be within the team, I consciously monitor and balance the ratio of energy expended externally on clients versus that expended within the business, and this should never drop below 80:20. The most successful salespeople operate at the highest ratio of revenue-generating activities every day. Should my revenue-generating activities drop below 80%, then I am not operating effectively to achieve my goals, and will inevitably get frustrated and burn out. I have learnt this the hard way, and companies that are poorly managed can fail on so many levels to keep their team focused on maximising their revenues. The 20% internal focus includes administration and all sales-related duties, such as team meetings, helping others and reporting to the Board of Directors. Selling to prospects has always been the easy part of my job but, in contrast, maintaining this ratio is the most important challenge I have ever faced. This is largely because I cannot abide and can easily rise to injustice, and this is rife in poorly managed sales teams where the management has little interest in, or understanding of, the criteria required to maximise the efforts of the team.

This section is dedicated to discussing some of the characters and obstacles that have directly affected my sales performance and the mechanisms that I have learnt to employ in order to deal with them.

GOOD MANAGERS, BAD MANAGERS

Top salespeople are notoriously hard to manage and, for some people, apparently I am no exception. A colleague once let slip that during a team meeting my boss was openly moaning about me. In my absence, he was explaining that I was a nightmare to manage and, when we next met, he attempted to excuse himself by joking about it. But it was too late – I had already heard and was baffled by his comments.

From my perspective, I was a point-and-shoot employee – give me a target and territory then forget about it. In my mind, all that my manager needed to do was protect me from internal distraction, add up my revenue every month and stick it in his monthly report. The only time he needed to spend with me was to sit down once a week to briefly discuss my revenue expectations for the month, as well as any client or competitive feedback that was appropriate to share with the team. For the most part, I did his job for him in terms of market strategy and hitting his team targets. When I explained this to him, he agreed that I had just described all the best points of working together, but there were a whole set of dynamics that were not so straightforward from a management perspective. A consequence of being so focused on achieving my personal goals was that I had a tendency to be insensitive to other people's way of doing things, which sometimes hurt the feelings of other, less successful, team members. Also, the constant positive affirmation that came from winning most of my deals led to me to think that I was always right. These attributes were apparently difficult to manage, particularly in situations when other salespeople felt that they had contributed, in part, to winning a mandate and were too intimidated to approach me to discuss a commission split.

My boss said he struggled to balance me with the rest of the team and didn't know how to get them to emulate my technique in order to be more successful. He further struggled not to be biased when allocating a larger expense budget to me than to everyone else and found this difficult to explain to his boss and other members of the sales team.

On further reflection, we seemed to spend most of our weekly catch-ups discussing his difficulty in integrating me into the team rather than revenue-generating strategies. These meetings were yet another complete waste of an hour and typically ended up in my being frustrated because, as a matter of habit, he would then take my strategies and present them to the Board of Directors as his own. Having forgotten where he had first heard it, he would often repeat my own ideas back to me in future meetings, as if he had devised some sort of strategic revelation. He would take every opportunity to hide behind his desk with administration and had no defined strategy as to how he was going to achieve his group target. He thought that complimenting my ability, then playing dumb, was an effective tactic to entice me to share my processes. It was boring and, despite having identified from the offset that he was useless to me, I took the job anyway because there was a clear path to my personal target.

In contrast, I have been lucky enough to have had the opportunity to work with incredible bosses. The best of these viewed the issues of integrating a top salesperson into his team as one of the best problems he could ever have. He understood the dynamics of how to do it because he too was an exceptional salesman and had encountered the same issues himself during his career. He truly understood me, and it opened my eyes to the value a good boss could bring to the table. Our meetings were productive – he was one of the few people whom I loved having accompany me to see clients because we understood each other's technique – and as the Managing Director of the company he understood how to play the dynamic of seniority to offer the client comfort and to close the deal. Our meetings were short, productive, and always based on generating maximum revenue, as there was total trust in each other's ability. He spent most of his time supporting and directing the sales team as well as interfacing with clients to ensure that our product offering was current and evolving.

This boss understood the challenges I faced and sought to remove all obstacles that hindered our mutual success. He led by example, shielding me from internal politics and allowing me to focus close to 100% of my time on the job. He often explained that he had to consider the team as a whole and made a conscious effort not to show any favouritism. We had become good friends, yet both respected the line between business and friendship. We were making a lot of money together so it was a nice problem to have, and his issues were not the minutiae of the other employer. He explained to me that the most difficult part of managing me was to manage my own expectations of the company, because if I was not happy, then the whole team felt it. The team looked up to my example and, if I disagreed with a certain company decision or new feature in the product, then the team tended to agree with me, which had an adverse impact on morale. It was a small price to pay, though, and being the smart guy he was, he often used this to help motivate the team by involving me at the early stages of such decisions and getting my support before announcing them to the rest of the team. To this boss I was a dream to work with that needed little managing. It is amazing to experience the difference between the two.

It is very difficult to understand which type of boss you are talking to during the interview phase. A good way to assess their sales acumen is to ask questions around their plans for the product and team, how they have set price points and group targets and where they think the soft spots are in the market that will generate the most revenue. They have targets for the team's success and it is important to agree on the overall strategy to hit these targets. If the interviewer cannot easily articulate how and where they will generate most of their revenue, it leads me to think that they are not in touch with the market, a consequence of this being that it is unlikely that I can rely on them to make good decisions on pricing or have an informed opinion should there be any dispute over territories and commission.

For example, a dispute may arise when catching a colleague encroaching on my assigned territory or account without telling me, and then playing dumb. A typical excuse might be that someone in their assigned territory knew the person in my account and sent an email introducing them because they had a deal for us. The correct protocol in this case, and one which a good manager would follow, is to reprimand the salesperson both for calling into my area and for not telling me. The salesperson is acutely aware that they are doing wrong. Now the business looks unprofessional because the company needs to explain to the prospect that there has been a mistake, and that the correct person to deal with is, in fact, me. Bad managers dismiss this behaviour as a mistake or no big deal. The problem with doing this is that, if you blur the boundaries in a team of experienced salespeople, then it leads to bad feeling and a breakdown of trust. Indeed, if this behaviour is rewarded, I consider that there is nothing stopping me from calling into everybody else's accounts. I did this once just to make a point and, of course, it led to disaster. A good boss would never tolerate this and their team operates with clarity, observing the necessary boundaries to focus on their assigned territories.

The most extreme case I have ever heard of with regard to lack of trust in a management team, was with a massive ticket deal that had the potential to generate several million in revenue for one particular company. The salesperson who had won the deal had so little faith in either her boss or the company to pay the commission that would be due that, despite her contract, she took extra steps when closing the deal to negate any risk of losing potentially several hundreds of thousands in commission to untrustworthy management. So she had her client, who had awarded the mandate, call the company directors and insist that they sign a document which stated that the salesperson responsible for managing them would be awarded the commission for the deal, because it was solely her relationship that won the mandate. This agreement, which the company deliberated over for several days before eventually signing, kept the sales vultures from trying to claim a piece of the credit for her hard work and guaranteed fair reward for months of pitching and years of relationship building. For a situation to get so out of hand that both a client and salesperson needs to do this in order to ensure fair treatment is a total failure of management on every level.

Inter-company politics tend to follow sales success. It's a fact that with seniority and experience come additional responsibilities and challenges. The top salesperson is always the target for those aspiring to take the title. As my book of business has developed in any given company, there has always seemed to be someone trying to jump on my deals or pitching to ease my workload. I think this is healthy, as long as the Sales Director controls and nurtures their ambition. Another consequence of sales success is that your opinion holds more gravitas and you are asked to contribute more to the running of the business and team. Again, this is great, but it can be time-consuming; the key is to give input without it taking up so much time and energy that it affects my sales results. The

80:20 rule is my way of monitoring the time it takes.

Good managers support and protect their team, have clear boundaries, are in touch with the market and can make informed decisions, manage sales dynamics and drive the success of each individual as well as the group as a whole. For me, they really add something that helps me to achieve my target and ultimately my personal goals. In a way they are unsung heroes because, if they are doing a great job, nobody tends to notice because they are taking care of the issues behind the scenes and allowing everybody else to focus on their jobs.

Bad managers are more noticeable, and I spend as little time as possible with them because they tend to drain me of time and energy, both of which are better channelled into sales. If they steal my strategies and ideas then that is fine, as it ultimately doesn't affect my earnings. But if they are using my ideas as part of their overall plan, then I see this as an opportunity to bend things in my favour by making suggestions that set or influence policies that work to my advantage. I used to get a little bitter when my boss took credit for my work, but actually it's far better for my own psyche to just let it go and keep sight of my personal goals. My saviour in times of need is always The Basics. These principles keep my focus in exactly the right place and drive the process of hitting my target, regardless of external stimuli.

INTERACTING WITH THE SALES TEAM

If I can't justify the actions of my peers or the company decisions, then I find it useful to detach emotionally from events and view my job as a game. Within the game are a set of players, each of whom are just doing their best to win and, as all players are not equal, in order to compete most develop styles that utilise their strengths to the greatest advantage. For example, some people are more emotionally astute than their colleagues and sell by emotionally connecting with their prospects, while others are more process-driven and consider the best way to win is to just do an exemplary job. Then there is a whole spectrum in between.

In order to succeed, the players in the game tend to develop two personas – the outward perception for the client and the internal personality to successfully interact within the company. In a highly structured sales environment, the sales team is governed by a defined set of rules and the characters are not free to develop in the same way as you will find in an autonomous environment. Remove boundaries, mix in the potential for high revenue-generating deals, and the team naturally finds its own balance with the most effective characters dominating. This can be an environment of constant and sometimes intense conflict, but the cream rises to the top by simply generating more revenue than their colleagues.

In one such team in which I worked, the management actually seemed to enjoy the conflict.

I always considered that having two personas must be exhausting, so am simply the same person internally within the company as well as externally in front of clients. I am also equally happy to work within either a structured or anarchic environment, just as long as two things are clear – first, that my key markers for product selection are met and, second, that I know the rules of engagement so that I can adapt my behaviour accordingly. Complete autonomy is not usually the most productive structure for a sales team, but it is the most lucrative for me, because I will literally expand everywhere.

What follows are some standout characters that I have consistently encountered, to a greater or lesser degree, in different sales teams throughout my career. The most pronounced examples of each are found in teams with little authority to govern behaviour but, regardless of where they lurk, they have cost me a lot of time, or money, or both. These people, and the games they play, are firmly on my radar to be avoided. Here, I not only want to expose them and share how they have affected my ability to achieve my target, but to also discuss how I have learnt to deal with them.

The Meeting Monkey

The Meeting Monkeys, as I call them, are total time wasters. As low to average sales performers, they are more focused on self-importance than personal financial gain. They spend their professional lives having "meetings" with just about anybody who will attend, and have no place in a new business sales team. They are typically very nice people who like to chat, so it can be hard to refuse a meeting, but once I label someone as a Meeting Monkey I am pretty brutal with them. They will use every tactic to book a time to discuss something menial that could be done by a short email, phone call or a simple question in passing.

A tell-tale sign of a Meeting Monkey is a hard spiral-bound book rammed with notes. They furiously write down everything you say, and I am sure this is to see if there is any content that they can use to sound intelligent in another meeting. Their game does work to some extent because what they really want is for me to do their job for them – maybe give them some market insight or tell them something new about sales. The highlight of a Meeting Monkey's week is the team sales meeting, because it's their chance to repeat what they have learnt from everyone else and it's the only legitimate meeting they ever attend. The fact is they are completely out of their depth and are just procrastinating because they don't have the mechanism, discipline or balls just to get on with it. Their goal is simply to survive, not to dominate or achieve.

One thing that fascinates me about Meeting Monkeys is that their diary never seems to have a slot. They have so many internal meetings booked that they will ask for a meeting, then suggest a random time two weeks in the future. In a way they are fascinating because if they made a minor adjustment to their behaviour, and booked the same number of external client meetings, then they would be in contention for the top sales spot. I don't know why it is, but they are client-facing averse and in my opinion better suited to sales support roles.

Meeting Monkeys seem harmless, but they are not. These characters have the ability to distract other salespeople into a broad spectrum of unrelated, non-revenue-generating issues and, once identified, they have little to no chance of ever pinning me down. If they come to my office and ask if we can sit down and discuss something, I say sure tell me now. If they won't and say we need to block some time out, I refuse. Denying a Meeting Monkey sometimes makes them panic and they get upset. If they keep asking, then my only available time slot is to walk with me to collect my lunch. It is surprising how many senior salespeople are Meeting Monkeys. They became senior by creeping to management and hanging around for several years, after which they are considered just part of the furniture. Whatever their motivation, good luck to them as long as it is their time that is wasted and not mine.

If a Meeting Monkey happens to be involved in a deal I am pitching, for example because one of the decision-makers happens to fall into their territory, then I just take control and invite them to the client meeting with me. Far better to ensure we win the business and give the Monkey their undeserved credit for it, than have them mess it up because Meeting Monkeys tend to be poor at actually selling.

The Box Monkey

The Box Monkeys are closely related to the Meeting Monkeys and, in extreme cases, the same person can be both. Their internal persona is that of the self-professed deep thinker who spends most of their time trying to think out of the box. They use corporate jargon like "let's play a game with this" or "imagine there is no such thing as a stupid idea". These characters thrive off the more junior salespeople whom they "take under their wing" and nurture. These inexperienced salespeople are the only people in the team who can't tell the Box Monkey to go away, and in some instances these characters are often able to convince the junior salespeople that they are almost god-like, even in the absence of any sales success.

The first mention of "the box" and my bullshit radar is spinning. These characters seem to confuse their sales role with studying for an MBA, and read endless self-improvement books for the latest techniques to share at sales meetings. They like to talk about thinking outside the box without ever actually knowing what the box is. I openly attack Box Monkeys at every opportunity because I just don't want to hear it. Creating this objectionable air towards them makes them less inclined to bother me. The fact is the only box they need to be thinking about is the one where they stop terrorising others with corporate drivel and get on with selling. My box is the section of this book called The Basics, and this has proven more than adequate to succeed in sales. Like Meeting Monkeys, Box Monkeys are procrastinators who, in my opinion, are positioning themselves as great lateral thinkers either to hide their insecurities about facing clients, or because they have ambitions above their station. The box, or The Basics as I call them, are tried and tested rules for generating product sales. Most of these so-called mavericks just can't follow them so they spend their time trying to be different rather than just getting on with it. Why? Because it takes discipline, which they seem to lack.

Box Monkeys like to consider themselves natural leaders. They often try to assume a position of authority and yet are either peers or more junior in stature, revenue and ability. I used to pacify them by listening to their ideas in the hope that they would go away. Big mistake, because Box Monkeys tend to have a bigger agenda and are not harmless. They are in the ear of management trying to put some of their ideas and observations into practice. So giving them any airtime or a shred of support for their proposals can distract in any number of ways from my personal targets and goals.

Let me give you a good example of a Box Monkey. I worked with a chap who was a decent salesperson and more often than not ahead of his sales target. This made him an interesting Box Monkey because he wasn't client-facing-averse. He sat second on the sales board, a good way behind me, just where I liked him, because I enjoyed showing him that his lateral thinking wasn't nearly as effective as just getting on with it. He was however desperate to be seen as the top salesman despite having no chance within his natural lifetime of taking the spot from me. So he constantly sought political affirmation and was always working behind the scenes to assume seniority over me and the team.

He kept bringing motivational ideas to senior management, and one time the board of directors succumbed to his request to hold a masterclass with each member of the sales team on how to achieve sales success. The premise was to teach people to break a tiny piece of wood and, in order to do so, they would have to see *through* the wood, which concluded with the revelation that the wood represents their sales target. The class took an hour per person and, somehow, this was supposed to motivate people. He approached me and asked my opinion, so I told him that it was stupid and that I didn't need motivating, especially from the second most successful salesperson. A board director, however, told me that he would really appreciate my attending in order to show support to the team, so I grudgingly agreed just to make the problem go away. I wasn't amused but ticked the box and suffered the seminar. Then it emerged that this Monkey has been granted an hour-long slot every week to motivate the team covering a range of topics that he had learnt from a book. That's an hour a week that I would never get back, so I categorically refused to attend and found myself either having to engage in a rapidly escalating dispute for directly disobeying the board of directors, or suffering this time-wasting fool.

I am absolutely not opposed to creative problem-solving when faced with a genuine sales-related issue. But, in relation to this chap, all he needed to do was focus on his job which was to sell more and motivate himself to overtake me on the sales board. A consequence of his lack of focus was a total waste of my time and a fight I had never had before. Thanks, Box Monkey... what an incredible asset you are!

The Leech

The Leech is your best friend in the sales team, sometimes. They predominantly exist in sales environments where there are multiple decision-making parties within a mandate, so more than one salesperson shares responsibility for covering the various prospects. Typically funny, cool, great on a night out, liked by everybody, and an average to decent salesperson, but lacking the killer instinct to be the best. They are astute enough to recognise their inadequacies and so adapt to compensate. They understand that they must make themselves useful to the top salespeople because without a "use" they wouldn't get airtime. They are always there to "help" with deals and can be relied on if you need something sales-related done at the office.

The Leech is a highly manipulative political animal and, through spending time with the top salesperson, they ensure that they feed back, behind the scenes, to management that much of your work is a result of their efforts. They are in their element with a weak, ill-informed boss whom they can befriend and manipulate. Another trait of The Leech is that they spend more time creating special bonds with internal players than they do selling to clients. These relationships, which blur the line between business and friendship, are key to the bigger plan.

The Leech has an agenda and is shrewd enough to know

that feeding off a big kill is worth far more than a number of small kills. They wait until a massive deal appears before showing their true colours, then go for a far bigger chunk than they deserve. When the deal is closed, their hard work behind the scenes pays off as their justification for a large percentage of the credit is bullet proof, despite the fact they did little but attend meetings where other salespeople did the work. Over the years The Leech has cost me more money than any other player in the game. It is possible to spot their game if you know what to look for, and they are most easily exposed when a large opportunity is on the table.

The first sign is if I catch The Leech reporting my work back to management, especially if we discussed it over a beer or off-the-record. Once suspicious, I consider a historical analysis of big deals that they have originated or led themselves. If there aren't any, then I ascertain whether the business they have signed to date always happens to be allied to a strong, independent salesperson. If they seem to have made a career from feeding off the efforts of others and it looks like I am the next mug in line, then it is time to cut the information flow and expose their game, in writing, to neutralise the inevitable claim. Having met quite a few Leeches over the years, I've noticed that they are all very quick to change allegiance once a deal is complete. So, if I suspect a Leech attack from my new best friend, then a reasonable question to ask myself is, where was this person prior to the deal coming about?

A genuine top salesperson in the making understands that if they are consistently originating and closing their deals independently, then sooner or later a big opportunity will present itself. The Leech is never going to achieve this status because they don't have the skill-set to generate business from nothing and operate alone. But depending on how good they are, their game can be very lucrative and often keeps them towards the top of the sales board month-on-month.

To demonstrate The Leech in action, there was a good size deal on the table but a small and ineffectual proportion fell under this particular Leech's territory. It was a complex process that required convincing multiple decision-making parties and, despite his spurious link, The Leech asked me if he could join in my meetings just to improve his sales skills. I agreed and thought nothing more of his reporting everything that had happened back to management shortly after each meeting. After all it saved me the effort, but what I didn't know was that he was presenting it as largely his own contribution. After a long and drawn-out process, the deal finally fell in my favour and he asked for a percentage. He told me that he thought his contribution was around 10% but hoped we could split this deal 50:50 on this occasion. This happened over a beer and, considering him a friend, I agreed on this occasion because he needed the credit to hit target. What I couldn't have foreseen was that this deal was the precursor to a much larger deal with the same client some months later and, throughout the process of closing the next tranche, The Leech was pitching internally to receive a further 50% of this too, despite having no jurisdiction or involvement. I only found out his intentions after the event and the management, who were completely out of touch, chose to support his claim. Despite my presenting irrefutable evidence to the contrary, this was one of the most unjust political decisions of my career and cost me several hundreds of thousands in revenue.

Having been stung so many times in my career, I – like all experienced top salespeople – will protect every single penny of my revenue ferociously. I never used to be like this, but characters such as The Leech, in combination with a bad manager, leave little choice but to behave in this way.

The Confidence Trickster

My least favourite of all the characters is the Confidence Trickster. This is typically a senior sales person who has learnt their craft in a sales environment where poor behaviour has been rewarded. The Confidence Trickster has evolved from The Leech and, over the years, has learnt to be a very competent salesperson. But experience has also taught him or her that big deals offer big rewards, so he or she will strive to assert themselves into sales processes that are completely unrelated to them. The

Confidence Trickster will actively call your accounts with the aim of meeting your prospects and making a connection. They genuinely could not care less about the consequences and know, in the face of a poor or uninterested management team, that "it's better to beg for forgiveness than ask for permission". After all they have nothing to lose. They don't fear confrontation and will argue that they knew the prospect already.

When confronted, their brazen response can range from completely ignoring the person to laughing in their face. If cornered they have no compunction in telling a bare-faced lie that is so easily disproved that it's embarrassing for all involved, and they often act hurt when questioned by management. But the Confidence Trickster feels no shame for their actions whatsoever because they know the damage is done. They are good salespeople who know how to make an impact in just one meeting, making it difficult for the correct person to take over. The Confidence Trickster has spent years refining their game and, because they have proven to be able to close big business, they know the company will not be likely to tell them to back off after the event.

Over the years, I have had a complex relationship with Confidence Tricksters because I have always found it difficult to accept that an astute salesperson, working alongside myself in the same team, can be a total write-off. These people are an enigma to me, because to be

THE NO.1 BEST SELLER

able to close big deals suggests they must have a level of emotional intelligence and therefore the ability to connect with people. So on the odd occasion where I have detected evidence of these woeful characters, I have endeavoured to connect with them and plead with them to align efforts, as it's just not productive or professional to disregard each other. This has never once proven successful because they are genuinely unbalanced and have absolutely no moral compass whatsoever. I could be having a cordial conversation with a Confidence Trickster at the coffee machine and two minutes later they would be calling my clients.

The Confidence Trickster doesn't hide. They are not friends with anyone in the team because they have trodden on everybody at one time or another. They just ignore all the bad feelings and don't care what people say because they know it will pass. They are difficult if not impossible to work with, and their actions can be very damaging to the business, the team morale and importantly to my earning potential, as their actions can take a lot of unnecessary effort to recover from.

I can't decide if Confidence Tricksters are very smart or really dumb, but in my eyes the way they conduct themselves is not something that I aspire to. I always felt a bit sad for them living such a negative existence, but my sympathy soon reaches its limit when they disrupt my work. These characters have cost me a lot of energy and money over the years. They can do real damage and have little interest in the consequences of their actions.

Dealing with them requires a three-pronged attack. Firstly, refusing to engage with them on any level, I make it clear that stepping into my business will instigate an equal if not more severe retaliation. This has little direct effect but, if the top salesperson creates enough of an issue about something, then management tend to take notice. Secondly, the only stimulus the Confidence Trickster responds to is money, so I push to have the commission structure changed to penalise poor behaviour. This should be par for the course for all sales teams, but it sometimes isn't and I have heard some idiotic justifications from managers as to why they don't penalise the Confidence Trickster, ranging from wanting them involved in every big deal because they have a strong track record to explaining that the team has always operated like this and has never had a problem historically. If the management team has been in place for a long time and is stale, then they don't know any better, so you are asking them to change to a doctrine they don't even know exists. In this case, to highlight the problem, it has sometimes been necessary to behave poorly myself to instigate a sanction against my own actions, and then after the event make sure this applies to all members of the team. This is a total waste of my time and effort, but in the face of weak management is the only way to have them respect their own boundaries.

If these two things are a lost cause, my third tactic is to get the Trickster hired-out. Every time a headhunter calls, I explain that the perfect person for the role is sitting 20 feet from me. In addition, I actively contact headhunter friends and recommend them as a good candidate to relocate. These characters can be difficult to get rid of because a good interviewer can recognise the telltale signs of a Confidence Trickster. Also, one of their common traits is that they have worked at the same company for many years and have spent this time manipulating the management team to accept their behaviour. This makes them apprehensive to move because they know that a well-run sales environment with clear boundaries would never tolerate their behaviour. Aside from having no choice but to deal with the fallout of the Confidence Trickster, it helps me not to engage with them emotionally by working towards their exit from the company as a whole.

It is not uncommon to find traits of each of these four characters in the same individual as, over time, members of the same team fall foul of the various dirty tactics and adopt these skills to their own game. Whether you can identify with them or not, the purpose of sharing their game is to make the point that I am always mindful of those with a vested interest in my work. It's not paranoia, but it is easy to become a victim of the many distractions and tactics employed by others to survive in a driven sales environment. Being an extreme person as well as someone of moral substance, I have engaged with, and fought, every one of these characters over the years, but the truth is that the clash of heads has never served me. I have had to ask myself, "What am I achieving from these clashes?" To show them how ineffective or revolting they are? Even if I achieve this, it amounts to nothing but a waste of effort. I have had to temper my instincts in order to co-exist and preserve my energy for the only thing that matters: my personal goals. And so it helps me to view these interactions as a game and, by doing so, focus my efforts without carrying detrimental emotional baggage.

OPERATIONAL SUPPORT TEAMS

The sales team bridges the gap between the prospect and the company by introducing the product or service, setting expectations, and communicating the client's requirements back to the support teams that then take over when a deal is agreed. Our jobs are intrinsically linked to one another and I need to have confidence that my teams can deliver on my promises. Integral to this process is the Operations Director. These people can be a best friend or a worst nightmare, but the fact is without each other we don't have a business.

It is imperative in a pressured environment that I work with the same set of people, who understand what I expect and how I go about my business. If there is anyone in the office who I see value in spending time with, it is the customer service team. Although we are all friends, there is a clear social and professional boundary, and I insist that they deliver nothing less than exceptional service. These teams are also a critical source of invisible revenue, and I like to have regular communication to ensure things are progressing smoothly. This is made much easier by working with the same group of people as this allows me to train them to recognise potential revenue opportunities that might not otherwise be picked up. I also like to involve the support team in relevant client meetings so that they understand the importance and urgency of their work, and also what it is that we do that gives us an edge over the competition. This is clear-cut, but there is one thing that can disrupt this, and that is the ego of the Operations Director.

For one reason or another, I have met several who simply don't like, or are threatened by, salespeople working too closely with the customer service team. A consequence of this is that they strive to be obstructive in order to assert their authority. If there is any fight that I am going to rise to, it is this one because it can have a seriously detrimental impact on the service we provide.

As a business grows, processes and policies are necessary to ensure the smooth running and reporting of activity. However, I have had occasions where customer service managers have attempted to stop the sales team from speaking directly to the support team, seeking to put policy in place that states we cannot communicate without their permission. It's petty and ultimately, as the top salesperson, I can blast through them by going over their heads, but it's such a shame. Nobody is going stop me from getting a real-time update on a deal that I spent months pitching for. The Sales Director should be managing this situation but they don't always do this. If I sense that the business is moving in a direction that results in a lesser service, then I set to oppose it and find a compromise, because working as closely as possible with my support teams and nurturing them to over-deliver has been key to my consistent sales success. I always take time for both the Operations and Customer Services Directors, to ensure we are on the same page and reassure them that I am not trying to circumvent them or do their jobs. After all, if either of these teams makes mistakes, then it's my pay cheque that gets penalised and an open line of communication is the best way to ensure that doesn't happen.

I used to make a point of having a beer with the customer service team every Friday after work. We worked hard all week and it was a good way to discuss any issues in a non-formal environment. There would be any number from the four people I used to work closely with up to 20, depending on whether or not my credit card was behind the bar. Many of the customer service team expressed an interest in working in sales and we often discussed how deals were won, but one evening in particular the conversation came around to what makes one salesperson better than another. Specifically, we were discussing why my counterpart in a different sales division was so aggressive towards them during deals.

One of team told me that they were scared to make the slightest mistake through fear of this particular salesperson's response. I explained that this was one of the contributing factors to his being a top salesman – because the customer services team were now extra diligent on his deals, and that was one of the reasons his clients had confidence in him. It was also why his results were so consistent, because he not only delivered a better service than the competition, but also than his own colleagues. He simply cared more than anybody else and made the support team raise their level to match his own.

He was an amazing salesman who I worked with closely and knew well. I explained that he was aggressive because he was under enormous pressure, not just from clients but from himself. He was under his own pressure to perform, maximise his revenues and provide an exemplary job. His work needed to be better than anybody else's because he knew that this was one of the factors in securing a flow of future business. He was driving excellence and the highest standards in the business, which in turn, was passed on to them.

To make my point, I suggested that we ran an experiment. I would send an email to this particular salesperson's entire team, offering a free lead on a first-come, first-serve basis. Bear in mind it was nearly midnight so no one would be sitting at their desk. We had a wager on who would reply first, but it was easy money because I knew who it would be. The email went out to eight salespeople and within 20 seconds I had my first reply. Two minutes later I had another and a couple more trickled in over the next hour or so. The winner was, of course, the top salesman in the team whom I knew checked his emails obsessively and never turned his phone off. We regularly exchanged emails well into the early hours of the morning and I explained that I could always reach him because he was always working. His clients had the same experience, and as we worked in a high-intensity, deadline-driven industry where our clients regularly worked through the night, they knew that if they were working with either this salesman or me then they were always supported. The team now took comfort that the demands of this salesperson were not personal, but motivated by good intentions and the interest of the business as a whole. Working with him was now seen as a learning experience, rather than met with dread.

Spending time with the teams in this way is invaluable, not just to encourage and educate them, but also to thank them for their contribution. It promotes a better working environment, and I consider that leading by example is part of a top salesperson's responsibility.

THE PATH TO BURNOUT

Business is booming, you are travelling to multiple countries a week, hosting deals and pitching relentlessly to maintain momentum, and all free time is spent entertaining clients with rich lunches, boozy dinners and sporting events. Sleep is far from your mind and you are firing on adrenaline because the commission is stacking. You constantly drink coffee and eat chocolate to maintain energy levels and your beautifully tailored suits begin to feel a little tighter. It doesn't matter because you are making the most of the current opportunity and nothing will stop you. You are bringing in so much business that the vultures are circling and the various characters in your team are constantly trying to assert themselves into your revenue stream. Despite pleading for intervention, your boss won't manage it. Then, you win a large deal and are subject to an unjust commission claim or a change in company policy that detrimentally impacts your contribution. The corporate politics begin to grate on the emotions and you become increasingly embroiled in disputes that further detract from your goal. The answer, you think, is simple – to fight harder, keep your foot on the gas and smash through problems like you do everything else.

You are now fighting two fights. One to win deals and hit your goals, the other against an ineffective management who hide behind their desks and spend months avoiding issues that could be cleared up in 24 hours. You refuse to relent; after all it is now a moral battle against the people who are not only perpetuating the problem, but who are unfairly taking the credit for your contribution.

Months, sometimes years, pass and you push and push to no avail. You feel unappreciated and, dare I say it, a little bitter towards the company that you perceive has treated you so poorly. After all, you have stuck to your word and given them everything. Your drive to succeed, which once burnt so bright, has swung 180 degrees and, despite having the ability to win every deal you pitch, you have been broken by the injustice of the system. Only when you finally detach, do you realise how utterly exhausted and burnt-out you have become. It happens, and I am not alone in having experienced it.

However, it can be avoided, and the biggest crime is not to learn from it. The answer lies in keeping perspective and being able to separate what is important from what is not. It is essential to find a healthy work-life balance. Until my 30s I never felt any form of limitation and would never have believed that the path to burnout could apply to me. For this reason, I never recognised any of its signs and my actions only exacerbated it. This is the opposite of what should be done, and symptoms of burnout are a clear sign that I need some downtime. Symptoms such as constantly reaching for a sugar rush, drinking several cups of coffee a day or bursting out of my clothes, an overall sense of discomfort in relation to on-going issues, or a lack of interest in going to work.

When you are operating at maximum capacity, burnout can easily creep up on you, and it is not to be ignored. Maintaining a healthy balance, in some ways, seems contradictory because it takes time away from selling, but this is not the case because you are able to re-engage with a fresh, more productive mind and a better sense of perspective. I achieve this by taking time to get out in nature, eating correctly and maintaining my fitness so that I can perform better back in the office. You need to escape, and if I need a day off, or two, I take it. That day off might still be in the office, but I will take a mental break by cutting back to the minimum and focusing on lead generation, new strategy or admin. If I am stressed and too tired to work out, I just take a sauna, but the point is that I constantly assess my fatigue level and make sure it doesn't detrimentally affect my ability to perform.

Other aspects of my overall strategy, such as focusing on a personal goal and following The Basics, help me to free some mental bandwidth because many of my actions are already ingrained. By doing so much preparation in the early stages of selling a product, I ensure that my daily activities don't take a great mental toll, so I am able to focus more effectively on customising my approach in front of clients, and managing my response within the company. Having lived through burnout, I can confidently state that letting it take hold is a choice that a salesperson makes. You chose how you respond to external stimuli and whether or not to let them affect you.

The best salespeople are able to separate issues based on whether they detrimentally affect their ability to hit target, and they also have mechanisms either to dismiss them or turn them to their advantage. Throughout the course of my sales career, I have learnt that the most healthy and productive response to anything non-revenue generating is to keep a sound perspective on the bigger picture and let it all go over my head. It has also helped me to embrace the fact that I am just one part of a wider team, and that not all decisions will fall favourably in my direction. Adopting a strategy that expects otherwise, or one that attempts to sustain 100% effort all of the time, is utterly unrealistic; you need time to rejuvenate mentally, emotionally and physically. A good manager will help their highest producers manage their time and effort, but ultimately the responsibility for maintaining your health and wellbeing is your own.

CONCLUSION

This section began with one of my favourite quotes from Jack Welch. It defines a well-structured and productive sales team, where the behaviour of each member is dictated by how they are compensated. It also helps to explain the behaviour of a top salesperson, who is simply conducting themselves in a manner that maximises their revenues.

I have often heard it argued that top salespeople are not team players, but I have never really understood this. If they were incentivised to be team players, then they would willing be the "top" team players, but in a job where their sole responsibility is to generate as much revenue as possible, it is potentially detrimental to allocate their time elsewhere. Their contribution to the team is to hit target, which contributes a greater percentage of income than any other salesperson, which adds to the success of the business and percolates through to everyone who works there. It does not mean that they do not enjoy helping others or getting involved in other aspects of the business, it just means that they are clear about their job and responsibilities.

The reason I have such an affiliation to this quote is because it says so much about the person who said it. He shows why he is considered such an eminent business leader – by demonstrating a clear understanding of the intrinsic motivations of genuine salespeople and how to nurture them. He is able to do this because he too is a top salesman. This, in my opinion, is where many sales managers fail – they cannot manage a team of exceptional salespeople effectively because they do not understand what drives them. In its simplest form, the quote explains that good salespeople work to maximise their personal revenues, but it also describes how to manage the potential poor behaviour of others – simply by financially penalising it. A good sales manager still needs to enforce this and understand that if someone doesn't respond to this stimulus, then they are wrong for the team.

The reality is that all team members have a corporate responsibility to act not only for themselves, but also for the good of the company as a whole, and this includes encouraging and helping one another. It is difficult for the top salesperson because their input is normally coveted above that of the management, and so they must carefully balance the time allocated to peer support against that of their own earning potential and ability to hit target. I described earlier how I manage this by ensuring that my team contribution sits within my 20% non-sales time allocation – which equates to one afternoon a week. Smart management will support this behaviour, as happened in one of my previous roles, by offering the top salespeople a team bonus over and above their commission rate, so that they are not penalised for allocating more time to helping their peers.

There are many potential obstacles to sales success, and with experience comes the ability to manage them confidently. Navigating the sales environment is just one aspect, and it is how you choose to respond to these inherent challenges that matters. The best salespeople promote harmony in the team and have mechanisms to address or dismiss these challenges in a way that minimises their impact on hitting their goals. They also understand that it is very easy to criticise others, but actually it is most productive not to waste their energy doing so.

The next section discusses contract negotiation — the final piece of my methodology in support of a successful sales career.

Section 4

Negotiating a sales-based employment contract

When a great job opportunity presents itself, it is easy to let emotions cloud your better judgement and gloss over the terms of your future employment. The primary focus is on joining the business and, as salespeople are driven by compensation, there is a common assumption that, as long as the numbers stack up, then the rest will be fine. In many cases this doesn't result in a negative consequence, but sometimes an innocent oversight can have grave consequences both during employment and post termination.

An employment contract is a document that clearly reflects the expectations of the company as well as those of the employee, and it should be a great thing that protects both parties in the event of a dispute. No provision of the contract should be open to differing interpretations, but the problem is that legal language can sometimes bear a different construction to a lawyer than to a layperson.

The first thing I do with any employment contract is to send it to my employment lawyer for review. Seeking professional advice is not expensive relative to the cost of getting it wrong, and it is part of my process to get a non-biased and informed second opinion. A lawyer will not only check that the document both factually and legally represents what has been agreed, but they will also benchmark the employment terms relative to the industry standard for the job that is being performed. In the past, I have received documents ranging from 6 to 23 pages – all for performing essentially the same set of duties. The latter contained obligations that were more appropriate for a company board member and my lawyer spent some time negotiating it back to something more appropriate for a senior salesperson.

The first time many employees discover inaccuracies in their contract or the legality of their obligations is normally when it's too late. Indeed, my own blasé approach has also led me to learn, first hand, some of the finer points of employment law. Here are some of the less obvious contractual clauses that have affected me detrimentally in the past and how I have dealt with them since.

1. RESTRICTIVE COVENANTS

Restrictive covenants, in the context of leaving a firm, are the employees' post-termination obligations. In a sales capacity, these covenants are more commonly known as gardening leave, non-compete and non-solicitation clauses. They protect the company by prohibiting the employee from dealing with customers, soliciting staff or competing in any detrimental way against the company for a defined period after the employee has left the business.

The length of gardening leave is normally proportional to the seniority of the salesperson and the potential damage they are able to do. For the latter part of my sales career, I have been subject to very lengthy gardening leave periods. Gardening leave is paid absence, so the employee is still effectively employed and can still be called upon to perform any of their duties as laid out in the employment contract. It is a very effective way of neutralising a salesperson and, from a company's perspective, it is understandable. The question is how long is reasonable to safeguard the business, without crippling the salesperson's ability to earn? Having sat out two 12-month lockout periods, I can vouch for the fact that it is an awfully long time and completely unnecessary. Paid absence sounds like a great deal. It is if there is a project that needs completing such as writing a book. However, as I have described in earlier chapters, there are a number of things that can happen in 12 months, such as a market crash or inter-company changes.

The other problem with gardening leave is that the salesperson is typically only paid their basic salary and not commission, which for me has always led to a substantial loss in earnings. Gardening leave is often followed by non-compete and non-solicitation restrictions, which are unpaid absences. For example, during my second 12-month absence, six months were paid gardening leave and the following six months were simply covered by a non-compete restriction, which barred me from joining a competitor. As this second six-months was unpaid, I agreed with my new employer that they would compensate me for my loss of earnings by paying me a golden hello the first day I joined. This one-off payment made sure I wasn't an entire year out of pocket simply for changing firm. After spending my second entire year out of the industry, I made the decision never to agree to a 12-month restriction again. Six-months, in my opinion, is more than adequate for a senior salesperson to be out of work and, if the company has a problem with this, they shouldn't have given me reason to leave in the first instance.

Restrictive covenants are a contentious issue and lawyers seem to have differing views on their enforceability. The fact is, if at any point I am deemed to be in breach of my restrictions then the liability is mine alone. I save myself the grief and legal fees by agreeing to a term that I think is reasonable before joining, and then stick to it.

2. DISCRETIONARY COMMISSION

Commission, to me, is not discretionary. I work to generate an agreed revenue number from an assigned territory and, when this is achieved, I get paid an agreed percentage of the revenue. There can be other incentives and benefits, but this is the nucleus of what sales means to me, and the performance-related pay model is one of the main reasons I love my profession.

In relation to this, there are some standard terms in sales contracts that are not acceptable. The most common of these typically comes immediately after your agreed commission structure and reads, "all bonuses and commission are solely at discretion of the company". This basically means that, if the company feels like it, everything that has just been written means nothing. Of course companies like to include this statement, but there needs to be some middle ground. I don't work as hard as humanly possible just to have my reward altered on a whim. This clause is unreasonable and I have my lawyer change it to "the company reserves the right to periodically review salary based on actual sales results". If this isn't acceptable to the company, then I want to document all the scenarios in which my commission would not be paid. This is far fairer, and if it is contentious then alarm bells ring.

3. CONTRACT DATES

The process of getting hired can take months, but shortly after employment terms have been agreed, they are written up to formally reflect the expectations of both the company and employee. On one particular occasion my contract was a short document that read quite simply. I was invited into the office for a quick skim of the terms, before heading out for dinner to celebrate. I glanced over the commission percentages and didn't hesitate to scribble my signature.

Some days later I re-read the contract and noticed a few discrepancies from what was agreed, with one mistake in particular needing immediate correction. The percentages for my commission were correct, but the dates that applied to my commission payments were wrong. I brought it to the company's attention and was told not to worry. I pushed to have it corrected and nothing seemed to happen, so I pushed harder. Then, just over half way through the sales year, I was asked to attend a meeting where it was explained to me that the management had reviewed my contract and couldn't agree on all the points, so it needed to be revised.

The result of my oversight led to a legal, political and commission-based disaster. It was a harsh lesson in paying attention to the smallest details of my contract before signing.

4. POOR EXECUTION

There was once an unfortunate situation that completely restricted me from selling into my assigned accounts. The company for whom I worked had a confidentiality breach, whereby one of the employees leaked some highly confidential information to someone in my largest account. She had taken this information from the internal database, and the result was that two of my four global accounts blacklisted us as an untrustworthy firm. The directors failed to act and I, through no fault of my own, was now unable to sell my products into 50% of my territory. I have since run this scenario through with any prospective employer and make sure this topic is accounted for in the contract.

Similarly, when selling service-driven products, I also look for written assurances of what will happen should the company poorly execute my deals. I can win the business, but I then rely on my support teams to complete the work. Any number of mistakes can happen that will damage my ability to charge a premium or secure future business, and I want to document what to expect in a worst-case scenario. This discussion also tells me a lot about the business and how they will conduct themselves when faced with adversity.

5. JOB DESCRIPTION AND TITLE

Is my contractual job description and title correct? I never cared about my job title and was never precious about doing someone else's job, just as long as the results were achieved. I also never considered that a true contractual reflection of my title and duties might matter, but it does, and there are two occasions where it can come back to haunt – in the event of a dispute, and post-termination with future employers.

It is difficult to visualise professional disputes before joining a company, but, particularly in large corporations that tend to be politically driven, disputes sooner or later affect everybody. This is when clarity of role and position are important. The job description describes the boundaries of the employee's responsibilities and is the default document in the face of a disagreement. If it doesn't truly reflect the role being performed, then your position is tenuous.

For example, the company may come to recognise a lazy or complacent sales manager and put his job in jeopardy. In an attempt to justify their contribution, the accused then turns on those who were picking up the slack, stating that they are operating out of their job roles. Following the official company procedures, this then goes through independent adjudication, and the default document upon which to make a verdict is the employment contract.

An inaccurate reflection of job title and duties can also come back to haunt you several years after leaving a firm. A future employer who seeks historical references will receive this information from the HR department of the previous employer. If the job specifics don't tally with what is written on your CV, then it looks like you have exaggerated your position. I experienced this once and it is an extremely uncomfortable and frustrating conversation. This is all down to not being bothered with the small print.

6. RENEWALS

It is important to look past the first sale and be contractually clear as to how these are viewed by the company.

For example, if I sell the same product a second time, to the same client, is it regarded as a renewal of business and paid at a different commission rate, or is it viewed as two separate sales? Also, what will happen if I sign a three-year deal with a 10% uplift year on year, or a multiple unit deal? Will I be paid on the total revenue accrued and, if so, when? I have fallen foul of this before by selling multiple units into a single account, which resulted in my company being awarded a "preferred supplier" by this client. My employer then argued that business was flowing from this account without my involvement and so my commission should be reduced. In effect, this client had become a "house account", though of course the only reason it was a house account is because I had made it one, so I failed to see how I had little involvement. There are a lot of little tricks companies can use not to pay out on commission, and being wise to these manoeuvres, I want the formula to be clear and accounted for in my contract from the offset.

7. COLLECTIONS

Companies differ in their definition of a closed sale and this can sometimes be used as an excuse not to pay the commissions due.

For example, some companies consider a sale to be complete, and therefore counting toward your sales-target, on receipt of a signed contract. In contrast, other companies tally the revenue when the client is invoiced. Finally, it is common when larger sums of money are involved that a deal is only considered closed when payment is received. This variance means that the time-frame between sending the invoice and it counting towards your target can greatly differ if you consider that some invoices have 30–90 day payment terms.

Many commission payments are dependent on hitting targets, but consider having an annual target and signing a deal in month eleven. The company will only count the deal towards your target on receipt of payment, yet the invoice has 30-day payment terms. You need this deal in order to hit target and get paid any commission for the entire year. You have a signed contract and plead with your managers but they refuse to commit to paying-out on commissions due. You know the client will not be in any rush to pay despite trying to incentivise them to do so, and pushing them any harder would be unprofessional. You have worked the whole year, this deal will put you substantially over target, and the associated revenues are the difference between a bumper pay cheque and nothing.

This is a nightmare scenario, but I have seen countless salespeople suffer loss of earnings in this way. In my experience companies don't pay out unless they must, so this type of situation needs to be accounted for before signing the contract. Depending on the firm there can be goodwill, but I don't rely on it. Rather, I run this or an appropriate example through with my employer and then negotiate around it. In this instance a reasonable compromise would be that, if I were to close a deal, obtain a signed contract or letter of intent, as well as invoice a client within month 11 only, then I would be given an extension of my 12-month time frame to collect this revenue. The extension would simply be proportional to the payment terms set out within the invoice, so in the example above it would be 30 days from the invoice date. In this instance, as long as the client paid within their allotted time frame, the revenue from this deal would count towards my annual target and commissions would be paid in accordance with the terms of my agreement. Should the company agree that this is a reasonable compromise, then it gets written up by the company lawyer and inserted into the contract.

The type of compromise will differ by product and sales role, but the point is that I no longer just blanket accept terms without truly understanding how they could impact me in the future.

It may seem alien to take such a comprehensive approach before beginning a new job, but the fact is that good salespeople very seldom stay in the same role for their entire career. It is therefore important to explore every scenario to find the correct balance between protecting both parties in case of a dispute, or if you come to part ways. In my experience, a prospective employer's receptiveness to constructing a mutually beneficial agreement is directly related to how much they want you to join. Some companies, notably large corporates, can take a totally inflexible like-it-or-lump-it attitude. However, most companies with which I have dealt are receptive to feedback. The key to finding a middle ground is to make reasonable compromises that protect both our interests and demonstrate a commitment to working together. If there is a reluctance to do so, then that is the company's prerogative, but at least you know what to expect and can weigh up whether the opportunity is really worth it.

Conclusion

Achieving sales success is, in my opinion, not about how you act when things are going well, but more about how you choose to respond when things are not. With a revenue number attached to your name, there is nowhere to hide, and it is the salesperson's responsibility to tackle the barriers and distractions that stand in their way. The most successful salespeople approach obstacles with an impenetrable self-belief that they will succeed. For me, this belief filters through every aspect of my role, from offering the best product and service to believing that my bill, which is seldom the cheapest option, is the correct fee for the premium service provided.

Being a top salesperson, however, requires something extra. It is not only an incessant drive or sense of higher purpose that comes from a personal motivation. It is also process-driven, and requires the ability to identify the correct product to sell, find a role that fits with your personality, apply a disciplined and technical approach to selling your product, and respond appropriately to external stimuli that can negatively impact your ability to maximise your earnings. When all of this is in place and the balance of probability is firmly tipped in your favour, it is finally about doing something different – a sprinkling of magic – that sets you apart from the crowd.

During my various tenures across different sales environments, I have noticed that integrity is often the attribute that separates the best from their peers. My reputation is worth more to me than that of my company, and I only ever viewed my role as a salesman as being an intermediary between the company and the client, placing the greatest importance on the latter. The knock-on effect of focusing firmly on my clients' needs is not just that I build concrete business relationships where others might have failed, but also that this mindset drives the company which I represent to provide the best possible product or service, as I insist that their internal procedures are of a standard based entirely on what customers are willing to pay for – a standard that, as we saw from Timothy in the introduction, is based on perfection.

A junior salesperson once asked me to describe my most memorable deal. The first thought that came to mind was from very early in my career. As a relatively inexperienced salesperson, I had just been assigned to cover Goldman Sachs, the biggest potential account in the industry.

Having attended a couple of preliminary meetings together with my boss, I was starting to really like the chap to whom we were pitching. These were not easy meetings because he was a very skilled buyer but, at the same time as negotiating the best deal for his firm, he was reasonable and had sound justification for everything that he asked. I had a great deal of respect for the way he conducted himself and was keen to show him that I was committed to giving him the most amazing service possible.

I was selling a database of documents that they used to research new acquisition targets. The volume of usage tended to fluctuate dramatically by month, and we had just released a new

> **❝ ...integrity is often the attribute that separates the best from their peers.**

set of content for this client to trial. Watching their usage like a hawk, I began plotting various schematic charts in Excel to share in our next meeting. These were the type of charts that I would have appreciated had our roles been reversed, because the decision-makers could get an immediate snapshot of how their team was using our system. After some months, enough data had been collated to calculate a reliable median usage trend and present a solid case to move from a transactional payment model to a contractual. It was the Holy Grail to contractually lock-down business with the biggest potential client in the world. I wanted to make it compelling, so I structured a deal that included a discount of 10% under the transactional median for a one-year commitment, or 15% for two years. I put all this in a beautifully presented document that my design team had collated. The deal structure accounted for median growth over the preceding two years, so I included usage uplift at current levels. Despite regular communication, we hadn't met for months, so I booked a face-to-face meeting to discuss my proposal.

This was a big deal for me and I wasn't quite sure what to expect. I was going alone for the first time and remember the buzz of pushing the heavy, iron revolving doors, before entering the reception area. In fact, I am reliving it as I type. I was ushered to the top floor and met by the Head of Department. We sat down and he explained how much he appreciated my efforts in managing his account and how well I had presented the data. The proposal had three options in it: a discounted wallet of data, which temporarily contracted them to us for a short period of time; a one-year deal at 10% median usage discount; and a two-year deal at 15% median usage discount. As our product was only being used in one team at the bank, I had also built in another incentive – that, if he committed to a two-year deal, then I would, at no extra cost, grant him the license to roll our product out to end-users, thus moving the workload from him to the people that he serviced.

I walked him through each item and he sat back in his chair and smiled at me. "What do you recommend I do, Lee?" he asked. I told him the truth – that the best deal on the table was option three as it not only offered the greatest saving but also relieved the workload within his team and allowed us, as a business, to invest in making sure that every single user was well-versed in the product over the following two years. It also safeguarded against the dramatic increase in transactional use that they might experience by increasing the product user-base tenfold. He said, "Fine, thank you very much. Send me the invoice later today. I will put in for payment this month." I didn't flicker. I held my hand out, told him how much I appreciated his business and thanked him in return.

The feeling of leaving that building, the excitement to tell my boss, the money I had personally earned from doing that deal, the trust and rapport I had built over the months, the fact that, within six months, I had just put a new product on every single desktop within the biggest bank in the world and that the renewal value after this term would be substantially higher than the current deal value, because there were tenfold users, all added up to as close to a perfect deal as possible. We were now in a position to receive product feedback from every end-user in the company and, going forward, could develop our system based on their exact requirements to ensure our new product was never off their desktops in the years that followed. This deal would, of course, also filter through the market to their peers and make selling to them a formality. I felt amazing, and this is the type of deal I try to emulate in every job and company for which I work. ***It's the type of deal that makes a top salesperson who they are.***

———

CONNECT

Feel free to drop me a line with feedback on this book or anything sales-related. I am always happy to connect with peers and review new opportunities:

Email
lee@leebartlettbestseller.com

LinkedIn
https://uk.linkedin.com/in/leebartlettbestseller

Blog
Join my blog: www.LeeBartlettBestSeller.com

Twitter
@no1bestseller

MY FAVOURITE SALES BLOGGERS ARE:

Jonathan Farrington
www.jonathanfarrington.com
Twitter: @topsalesworld

Jeffrey Hayzlett
www.hayzlett.com
Twitter: @JeffreyHayzlett

John Barrows
www.jbarrows.com
Twitter: @JohnMBarrows

S.Anthony Iannarino
www.thesalesblog.com
Twitter: @iannarino

Gary Vaynerchuk
www.garyvaynerchuk.com
Twitter: @garyvee

Grant Cardone
www.grantcardone.com
Twitter: @GrantCardone

Mark Hunter
www.thesaleshunter.com
Twitter: @thesaleshunter

Barbara Giamanco
www.scs-connect.com
Twitter: @barbaragiamanco

Jill Konrath
www.jillkonrath.com
Twitter: @JillKonrath

Keenan
www.asalesguy.com
Twitter: @keenan

Jeb Blount
www.jebblount.com
Twitter: @salesgravy

Ken Krogue
www.kenkrogue.com
Twitter: @kenkrogue

Brian G. Burns
iTunes: The Brutal Truth About Sales
Twitter: @briangburns

Will Barron
iTunes: Salesman Podcast
Twitter: @salesmanred

Hubspot Sales Blog
www.hubspot.com
Twitter: @hubspot

Tony J. Hughes
www.rsvpselling.com
Twitter: @rsvpselling

Jamie Shanks
www.salesforlife.com
Twitter: @jamietshanks

Matt Heinz
www.heinzmarketing.com
Twitter: @heinzmarketing

GLOSSARY

Account Manager: A type of sales role that is primarily focused on maintaining and growing pre-existing client relationships and sales channels.

Assumptive Close: A sales technique whereby the salesperson intentionally assumes a prospect has agreed to buy their product or service.

Basic Salary: The fixed proportion of a salesperson's total remuneration, before adding commission and other financial incentives.

Beauty Parade: A situation in which several companies are invited to pitch for a piece of business.

Burnout: The emotional, mental and physical exhaustion cause by excessive and prolonged stress.

Closed Questions: Questions that can be answered with a simple yes or no.

Closing Techniques: The set of sales techniques that lead the customer into making a decision.

Company Financial Year (FY): Sometimes referred to as Fiscal Year, this is the period that a company uses for accounting purposes and preparing financial statements.

Consultative Sales: A sales method that involves the salesperson taking time to understand the client's professional pain, and then recommending a solution that alleviates the problem.

Contractual Revenue: A pre-agreed revenue stream that relates to the provision of a product or service, and that is underwritten by a contract.

Discretionary Commission: A type of commission or bonus scheme that is paid at the discretion of the company.

Economic Downturn: A slowing or reversal in the rate of economic growth. Negative economic growth for two consecutive quarters is known as a recession.

Enterprise Sales Solutions: A type of sales that involves taking a broad view of a customer account and devising a strategy that sells one, or number of sales products across the entire organisation.

Entertainment Budget: The allocation of revenue for building and maintaining client relationships, with the intention of securing future business.

FTSE 100 Corporate: A company whose stock is amongst the top 100 most actively traded on the London Stock Exchange.

Gardening Leave: The period after an employee leaves a company in which they are still being paid. The employee is absent from the office, yet can still be called upon to perform their duties as per their employment contract. It is often applied when a salesperson leaves a company to join a competitor.

Golden Hello: A payment given to a senior executive to entice them to join a new firm.

Golden Parachute: A payment or financial compensation package that is payable to an executive should they be dismissed as a result of a merger or takeover.

IPO (Initial Public Offering): The name given to describe the first time a company opens its stock to be publicly traded on the stock market.

M&A transaction: A type of corporate transaction that refers to the consolidation or sale of a company.

MBA (Masters in Business Administration): A post-undergraduate degree program that focuses on multiple aspects of business, finance and management skills.

New Business Salesperson (NBS): A salesperson whose primary focus is to identify and establish new customer relationships that result in closing new business.

Open Questions: Questions that require a more detailed answer than simply yes or no.

Operational Support Team: The team(s) responsible for managing the client after a sale has been agreed.

Performance-Based Equity: Stock or shares that are offered or issued to a salesperson when their performance quotas are reached.

Physical Data Room (PDR): A confidential document collection that is housed in a secure physical location. Prospects wishing to access the documents are given a defined window in which to do so. In the context of a financial transaction, they are scheduled in a way to maintain their anonymity, and this adds time to the transaction process.

Pre-Close: A sales technique that asks for the business from a prospect, on delivery of any outstanding objections.

Private-Equity Owned: A private company that is owned by an investment house.

Privately Owned Company: A company that does not offer or trade its stock to the public stock market, but rather is owned and exchanged privately.

Probation Period: The initial period of employment where the company considers whether the employee is able to meet the expectations of their job role.

Procurement Team: The team in an organisation responsible for the purchase and acquisition of third-party products and services.

Product Adoption Curve: A graphical representation of the adoption or acceptance of a new technological product or innovation over time. It further categorises the various groups of adopters by type.

Project Name: An alias given to a deal or project to safeguard its identity.

Request for Pricing (RoP) document: A document used to invite suppliers to participate in a bidding process for products and services. It details the specific requirements of the buyer and defines the boundaries of the pitch process.

Restrictive Covenant: The section of an employment contract that prohibits an employee from competing with or soliciting customers from their ex-employer for a certain period post-termination.

Sales Territory: A customer group or geographical region that a salesperson is responsible for selling into. It can be defined by a combination of factors, but it describes the boundaries of a salespersons' allocated customer base.

Sales-Call Reluctance: A fear or avoidance of contacting prospects for the first time.

Sales-Cycle: The time between the initial contact with a prospect and the closing of a deal.

Sales-Pipeline: A list of potential customers who are graded by position in the sales cycle and probability of closure. It allows the salesperson to predict their expected revenue over various time frames.

Strategic Partnership Channel: A partnership between two commercial enterprises that is formed to take advantage of the independent mutual benefits of each.

Total Market Sizing: The revenue potential in any given market. This often includes an explanation of the total number of potential sales as well as a breakdown of the institutions and individuals who would be in a position to mandate future business.

Transactional Revenue: Revenue that relates to ad-hoc usage of a product or service.

Transactional Sales: A sale typically defined by a short sales cycle, and a set of fixed requirements upon which a customer will make base their selection.

Virtual Data Room (VDR): An online repository of information that is used to store and distribute confidential information. It keeps all users anonymous from one another and furthers allows the administrators to manipulate content, track document activity, and respond to questions.

Warm Referral: A sales call that is preceded by a positive introduction or recommendation to the potential customer.